DENVER DOSSIER

THEMED ADVENTURES FOR EVERY TRAVELER

TRAVEL

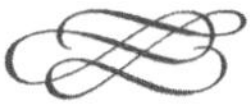

KIMBERLY BURK CORDOVA

TABLE OF CONTENTS

To the spirited souls of Denver, whose vibrant energy and warm hospitality make this city a beacon of community and culture. Your enduring spirit and unwavering resilience inspire us all. This book is dedicated to you, the heart and soul of the Mile-High City.

"Denver is a city where the air is crisp, the people are friendly, and the beer is cold."

— JOHN DENVER

INTRODUCTION

As the sun rises over the Mile-High city, it paints the sky in a stunning blend of pink and orange, signaling the start of a new day in Denver. This city, a kaleidoscope of one-of-a-kind experiences, is a treasure trove waiting to be unearthed. Every street corner and mountain trail has a story to share, like Larimer Square, a bustling marketplace during the gold rush, and Red Rocks Park, a natural amphitheater that has witnessed legendary music performances. The air is filled with the aroma of pine and the promise of gastronomic delights, from the famous Denver omelet to the daring Rocky Mountain oysters. Denver is a city that beckons you to explore, from its artistic heartbeat at the Denver Art Museum to the wonders of the Rocky Mountain National Park. As a Denver native, I'm thrilled to share these incredible narratives and experiences with you, inviting you to embark on your journey of discovery.

Hey there! I'm Kimberly, a Denver native and an avid traveler. Denver isn't just a city to me; it's a part of my identity. My love for this mile-high city has only deepened with my global escapades. I'm not just a guide but a fellow traveler who understands the thrill of exploring new places, the excitement of immersing in a different environment, and the wonder of experiencing a unique culture. My profound bond with Denver, nurtured through my upbringing and travels, ensures that your experience embodies the city's spirit. You can trust me to show you the best of Denver, just as I would for a dear friend.

This book is your portal to Denver's soul, a guide to its heart. Whether you're a lover of art, a connoisseur of history, an outdoor enthusiast, or a family searching for fun, I've crafted unique experiences for you in Denver. Each itinerary is a meticulously curated collection of experiences, promising an authentic and memorable exploration of Denver. With its many offerings, Denver always has something new and exhilarating to discover, catering to all ages and interests. Prepare to be spellbound by the city's vibrant art scene, storied history, and awe-inspiring natural landscapes.

I have designed this guide with everyone in mind, from families looking for fun to seniors seeking serenity to anyone curious about navigating the city quickly. I remember the first time I stumbled upon a hidden mural in RiNo, a vibrant neighborhood known for its street art. It was a moment of pure discovery, and I can't wait for you to experience the same thrill. I am thrilled that you will experience the joy of discovering Denver's hidden gems.

Get ready for more than just recommendations; this book is a comprehensive guide bursting with personal anecdotes, practical tips, and insider secrets that will have you navigating Denver like a seasoned local. From the best spots to catch a sunset over the city skyline to exploring our diverse neighborhoods, I'm handing you the keys to the city, ensuring your visit is as smooth and enjoyable as possible. With this guide, you'll feel confident and ready to explore Denver at your own pace, knowing you have all the information you need. This guide is your trusted companion, insider, and ticket to an unforgettable and well-prepared Denver experience.

So, consider this your thrilling invitation to embark on your Denver adventure. With this guide, you are a visitor and fellow explorer prepared to discover Denver's diverse experiences. Denver has a kaleidoscope of offerings, from art, history, and food to breathtaking outdoor landscapes. With its unique blend of traditional styles, seen in the historic Larimer Square, and contemporary styles, showcased in the modern architecture of the Denver Art Museum, you'll get a taste of our architectural diversity. We also have a rich history dating back to the Gold Rush, a diverse culinary scene, and beautiful outdoor landscapes. There's something for everyone to enjoy, and I can't wait for you to experience it all. Let's embark on this thrilling journey of discovery together.

DENVER'S ARTISTIC SOUL

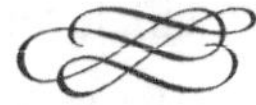

Nestled in the heart of Denver, the River North Art District (affectionately known as RiNo) is a neighborhood where the lively energy of city life harmoniously blends with pockets of artistic tranquility. Once overlooked and filled with industrial warehouses and factories, this neighborhood has undergone a remarkable metamorphosis. In the 1980s, a group of artists and entrepreneurs saw the potential in these abandoned buildings and began transforming them into art studios and galleries. Today, RiNo is a vibrant hub of art and culture, a testament to how community and creativity can reclaim and revitalize urban spaces. Art is not confined to galleries here; it spills onto the streets, turning the district into a living canvas where every wall tells a story, every gallery is a portal to inspiration, and every corner beckons visitors to explore Denver's dynamic artistic soul.

THE PULSE OF RINO: STREET ART AND GALLERIES

RiNo, is not just a Denver neighborhood but a living canvas for local and international artists. The murals and street art here are not mere decorations; they ignite conversations about society, culture, and identity. For instance, the 'Love This City' mural by Pat Milbery and Pat McKinney vividly represents Denver's spirit. A stroll through RiNo is an exhilarating journey of constant discovery, with each step unveiling a new piece of art. The district's open-air gallery of murals and street art transforms a simple walk into an immersive art experience, with each piece telling a unique story waiting to be uncovered by the curious visitor.

The indoor counterparts to the outdoor art spectacle are the galleries of RiNo, which offer a deeper exploration of artistic expression. They range from avant-garde showrooms featuring cutting-edge contemporary artists to cozy nooks housing traditional crafts and paintings. What truly sets RiNo's galleries apart is their warm and inviting nature. These spaces are not just for art enthusiasts; they are designed to encourage visitors of all backgrounds to interact with the art, creators, and curators who bring them to life. The accessibility of these galleries demystifies the world of art, making it approachable and enjoyable for everyone, ensuring that every visitor feels valued and included in the artistic community of RiNo.

Community engagement in RiNo is not just about appreciating art; it is about active participation in the district's ongoing narrative. Artists don't just contribute their work to the neighborhood's aesthetic but to its identity. There are numerous opportunities for locals and visitors to participate in workshops, public art projects, and collaborative spaces in the neighborhood. This participatory culture fosters a deep sense of belonging and ownership, forging a strong bond between individuals and the community. It's not just about being a spectator; it's about being a part of something bigger that enriches the individual and the community, making everyone feel connected and involved in RiNo's vibrant art scene.

One of the most exciting aspects of RiNo's art scene is the First Friday Art Walks. On the first Friday of each month, the district comes alive with a vibrant festival of creativity. Galleries like the **Ironton Studios and Gallery**, the **Plinth Gallery**, and the **Helikon Gallery** open their doors, welcoming diverse art enthusiasts, curious locals, and international visitors. The streets are filled with performances, food trucks, and pop-up art installations, creating a celebratory atmosphere that encapsulates the spirit of RiNo. These art walks aren't just about showcasing art; they celebrate the communal effort to maintain and evolve the district's creative soul. They provide an opportunity for anyone, regardless of their knowledge or experience in art, to fully immerse themselves in Denver's diverse and vibrant artistic community.

Explore RiNo's Street Art: A Self-Guided Tour

To explore RiNo's street art scene, consider embarking on a self-guided tour. Start your tour at the intersection of 26th Street and Larimer, where you'll find a cluster of murals that set the tone for what's to come. While wandering, check out the **Denver Central Market,** a hub for local food artisans with several iconic art pieces on display. Remember to explore the alleyways as well; sometimes, what might seem like a shortcut can lead you to hidden corridors of creativity, often housing some of the district's most striking works.

As you explore, be sure to venture into the galleries you pass. Each one offers a unique perspective on the art world, from contemporary to traditional. If you visit on a First Friday, adjust your schedule to arrive in the late afternoon when the festivities begin. This is when the true vibrancy of RiNo comes to life, offering an unparalleled experience of Denver's artistic heartbeat.

RiNo's story is one of transformation, creativity, and community. It stands as a testament to the power of art to rejuvenate and inspire not just individuals but entire neighborhoods. With its ever-changing walls and welcoming galleries, this district invites everyone to partake in its ongoing narrative, creating a collective experience that enriches both the visitor and the community. Through the lens of RiNo, we see not just the art of Denver but its heart and soul.

PUBLIC ART WALKS: A JOURNEY THROUGH DENVER'S SOUL

Denver's landscape is not just a backdrop but a living canvas that breathes life into the city's history, culture, and aspirations through public art. With its curious gaze into the Convention Center, the towering Blue Bear and the fiery-eyed Mustang at the Denver International Airport are guardians of Denver's artistic soul. These pieces, and many others scattered throughout the city, such as the *'Big Sweep'* broom sculpture in front of the Denver Art Museum and the *'Dancers'* mural on the side of a building in the RiNo Art District, are not mere decorations but are profound expressions of the city's identity. They serve as points of connection, drawing lines between past and present, between residents and visitors, and between the natural landscape and its urban heartbeat, inviting you to be a part of Denver's story.

Navigating Denver's public art collection is like embarking on a treasure hunt, where each discovery unveils a new layer of the city's narrative. The stories behind these artworks, often as captivating as the pieces themselves, are a testament to

the ingenuity and foresight of their creators. The Blue Bear, affectionately known as *'I See What You Mean'* by Lawrence Argent, playfully comments on the curiosity that defines human nature. Meanwhile, Luis Jiménez's *'El Mesteño'* embodies the untamed spirit of the West despite its controversial reception. Each piece beckons onlookers into a conversation, encouraging them to delve deeper and uncover their interpretations and connections to the city.

Exploring Denver's public art is not just a walk but an interactive journey. Self-guided and city-organized tours, accessed through a mobile app, provide a structured path through Denver's public art landscape. These tours are thoughtfully designed to showcase and contextualize the art within Denver's broader cultural and historical narrative. QR codes beside artworks link to stories of their inception and impact, bringing the artist's voice directly to the audience. Seasonal events organized by the city turn these art walks into communal celebrations, creating a living, breathing exhibition under the open sky. This interactive approach ensures that every step you take is a step deeper into Denver's art scene.

This intertwining of art and urban identity is no accident but a deliberate effort to weave Denver's values and aspirations into its visual landscape. Public art becomes a mirror reflecting the city's diverse culture, its resilience, and its dreams. It speaks of Denver's rich Indigenous heritage, pioneering spirit, and commitment to sustainability and inclusivity. The artworks dotting Denver, from its parks to its busiest streets, serve as markers of identity, creating a sense of place that is unique and unmistakable. They tell the story of a city that values creativity and community. It looks to its past to inform its future and sees art not as an accessory but as a necessity.

Accessibility is not just a concept in Denver's approach to public art but a core value that ensures culture is not a privilege but a right for all. The strategic placement of pieces in public spaces, free of charge, and the diversity of themes and representations are tangible efforts to make art a part of everyone's life. Programs tailored to engage individuals with disabilities, seniors, and those from economically disadvantaged backgrounds underscore the city's commitment to breaking down barriers to cultural participation. In Denver, art is a tool for unity, a bridge across differences, and a source of communal pride and cohesion, inviting everyone to share in its beauty. Your presence is valued and celebrated in Denver's art scene.

Public art is more than an aesthetic addition in this city where the mountains meet the plains. It is the pulse of Denver's cultural heart, a constant reminder of the city's evolving story, and an open invitation to all who walk its streets to pause, reflect, and connect. Through its public art, Denver reveals itself not just as a city of beauty but as a community that values expression, dialogue, and accessibility, holding art as a shared treasure for all to enjoy.

THE DENVER ART MUSEUM: A MODERN MARVEL

The Denver Art Museum (DAM) is a standout feature of Denver's cultural landscape. Its buildings, masterpieces in their own right, were crafted by the esteemed architects Daniel Libeskind and Gio Ponti. Libeskind's Frederic C. Hamilton building, with its striking geometric glass and titanium exterior, is a testament to the museum's connection to the majestic Rocky Mountains. Ponti's North Building, a treasure trove of the museum's collections, challenges conventional ideas of what a museum should be with its distinctive brutalist design, inviting visitors to reimagine their understanding of art and its presentation.

The museum treats visitors to a wealth of art, from ancient Indigenous artifacts to cutting-edge multimedia installations. The Indigenous art collection, one of the most extensive in the U.S., has garnered international acclaim for its depth and breadth. It weaves a narrative of creativity and resilience, showcasing pieces from various centuries. Contemporary exhibits feature works that challenge, delight, and provoke thought. The DAM's commitment to showcasing diverse cultures and perspectives positions it as a global player in the art world, offering visitors a glimpse into the vast, diverse world of human creativity and a chance to engage with art from around the world without leaving Denver.

The Denver Art Museum stands out by offering unique experiences that ignite a spark of curiosity and bring art to life. Interactive installations invite visitors to enter the art, blurring the lines between observer and participant. Digital experiences, from augmented reality tours to online collections,

extend the museum's reach far beyond its physical walls, making art accessible to all. These immersive exhibitions transform the museum from a place of passive observation to an active, participatory experience, sparking curiosity and fostering a deeper connection with the art. Your visit to the museum is not just a passive experience but an opportunity to engage and be inspired by art in ways you've never imagined.

The Denver Art Museum's commitment to educational outreach is a testament to its inclusivity. The museum has developed programs to bring art to all corners of the community, from school programs fostering early appreciation and understanding to workshops and classes opening the world of artistic creation to people of all ages. Partnerships with local organizations ensure that the museum's resources benefit the broadest possible audience, making art an accessible, integral part of the Denver community. Your presence and participation are not just welcomed but celebrated in the Denver Art Museum's inclusive art community. This commitment to inclusivity ensures that everyone, regardless of age or background, can find a place in Denver's art scene.

The Denver Art Museum becomes a testament to innovation and creativity as the sun sets. It is where art is observed and experienced, and community and culture intertwine. With its modern marvels, diverse collections, and engaging exhibitions, the DAM continues to chart a course for the future of art, inviting all who enter to join in its journey of exploration and discovery.

HIDDEN ART SPACES: DENVER'S BEST-KEPT SECRETS

In the heart of Denver, a network of art spaces beckons those seeking a unique journey of discovery. These hidden treasures offer a fascinating peek into the city's artistic pulse, from cozy underground galleries nestled in alleyways to lively artist collectives thriving in repurposed industrial structures. Each space boasts a distinct character and ambiance, inviting the adventurous to uncover a side of Denver that thrives in the shadows of its more prominent cultural establishments.

These clandestine venues serve as the lifeblood of Denver's art scene, empowering local artists whose voices might otherwise be drowned out in larger commercial spaces. Emerging talents find the freedom to experiment and express themselves, often pushing the boundaries of traditional art forms. The palpable support for these artists, from gallery owners to the community, is a testament to Denver's commitment to fostering creativity and innovation. It is a nurturing environment where artists can grow, collaborate, and thrive, contributing to a vibrant ecosystem that enriches the city's cultural landscape.

Celebrating cultural diversity within these spaces mirrors the city's mosaic of identities. Exhibitions and installations span a spectrum of mediums and themes, reflecting the myriad experiences and perspectives that make up Denver's community. From multimedia installations that explore contemporary social issues to traditional crafts passed down through generations, these art spaces act as a conduit for cultural dialogue. They encourage viewers to broaden their perspectives, promoting a deeper understanding and respect for our diverse world.

At the core of these concealed art spaces lies the community. They open their doors to the public with workshops, discussions, and events crafted to engage and inspire. On any given day, one might stumble upon a local artist leading a printmaking workshop, a panel talk on the influence of art in social movements, or a poetry slam that unites voices from all corners of the city. These events provide a stage for artists to showcase their work and create opportunities for meaningful interaction and collaboration among Denver's creative souls.

Navigating the labyrinth of Denver's hidden art scene quickly reveals that these spaces are more than just venues for displaying art — they are vital hubs of creativity, education, and community. They remind us that art is not a solitary endeavor but a collective expression of human experience. Through their dedication to backing local artists, embracing cultural diversity, and encouraging community engagement, these concealed art spaces enhance Denver's cultural identity, enriching the city in ways that extend far beyond their physical confines.

FIRST FRIDAY ART WALKS: WHEN DENVER COMES ALIVE

In Denver, on the first Friday of every month, the city comes alive with the First Friday Art Walks. These events, which feature a variety of activities such as live music performances, interactive art installations, food and drink tastings, and even art workshops for kids, showcase the vibrant art culture of the city and bring together artists, art lovers, and casual visitors to celebrate creativity, conversation, and collaboration. The art walks turn the districts of Santa Fe and RiNo into dynamic and living galleries, where every alleyway and storefront showcases the creative expressions of the city's inhabitants.

The accessibility of art during these walks is not just remarkable; it's a testament to Denver's commitment to inclusivity. Galleries that were once seen as exclusive spaces become welcoming environments where artists and visitors engage in dialogues. The democratization of art allows for a broader appreciation of creativity and fosters a sense of belonging among participants. These walks serve as entry points for many people to explore Denver's artistic community and contribute to the city's cultural enrichment.

Aside from their cultural significance, the First Friday Art Walks play a significant role in Denver's economy. These events, which attract a large number of visitors, bring foot traffic to small businesses and galleries, and the transactions during the walks contribute to sustaining Denver's vibrant art scene. But more than that, social capital is also generated through these events, fostering a deep sense of community pride and ownership that ties the local art scene's success to the city's well-being.

First Friday Art Walks also provide a dynamic platform for connection and collaboration among artists. These events encourage openness and allow artists to share their experiences, challenges, and aspirations with peers and enthusiasts alike. Emerging artists can find mentorship, support, and opportunities to showcase their work. Art lovers and collectors gain insight into the creative process and forge personal connections with the artists and their art. These interactions and collaborations benefit individual artists and contribute to Denver's art scene's overall growth and vibrancy.

The communal spirit of First Friday Art Walks epitomizes the ethos of Denver's art culture — open, inclusive, and vibrant. These events celebrate art and community, bringing together diverse crowds from seasoned art critics to families exploring the scene for the first time. They are a testament to Denver's unwavering commitment to its arts culture and ability to weave creativity into the fabric of the community, fostering a deep sense of community pride and ownership that ties the local art scene's success to the city's well-being. So why not join in the celebration? Plan your visit to Denver's hidden art spaces and mark your calendar for the next First Friday Art Walk. You won't be disappointed.

HISTORIC DENVER DELIGHTS AND ARCHITECTURE

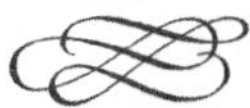

Denver is a modern city that values its historical heritage, blending it with contemporary elements to create a unique identity. The story of Denver is not just a series of events but a living entity that shapes the city's distinct character. The elegant Victorian houses in Capitol Hill reflect a timeless elegance. At the same time, the revitalized Union Station showcases Denver's ability to blend the old with the new. This fusion of tradition and innovation is an ongoing dialogue that enriches Denver's cultural and societal tapestry.

At the heart of Denver, the skyline offers a stunning view that echoes the natural beauty that surrounds it. It showcases a blend of human creativity and nature's allure, a testament to Denver's architectural ambition. Buildings in Denver are more than just structures; they are tributes to the city's rich history, its pursuit of progress, and the enduring spirit of the American West. With its shining golden dome, the Colorado State Capitol Building is a perfect emblem of this blend. It honors Colorado's rich heritage while looking toward a bright future. It stands out as one of the city's architectural gems.

THE MOLLY BROWN HOUSE: BEYOND THE TITANIC

The Molly Brown House is not just a museum but a portal to Denver's opulence, complexity, and cultural richness of the early 1900s. Its original furnishings and stunning stained glass windows are not just decorations but tangible links to the history that continues to shape Denver today.

Margaret 'Molly' Brown, a figure of significant influence in Denver, is more than just a survivor of the Titanic disaster. Her Victorian mansion, nestled in the heart of Capitol Hill, is a testament to her vibrant personality and her profound contributions to Denver's cultural and social growth. Did you know Molly Brown was among the first women to run for political office in Colorado? Today, the Molly Brown House Museum is a living tribute to her life, offering a unique window into Denver's history at the turn of the 20th century.

Margaret Brown's Legacy

The Unsinkable Molly Brown was a prominent Denver figure and a beacon of inspiration. Her philanthropy, social reform efforts, and visionary approach were admirable and transformative. She promoted women's suffrage, advocated educational reform, and fought for workers' rights, leaving an indelible mark on the city's development. The museum showcases her life in great detail, offering an intimate glimpse into her world and curated displays highlighting her legacy. Visitors can immerse themselves in the life and accomplishments of a woman whose legacy shines bright, not only because of her tragic past but also due to her significant contributions to society. This personal connection allows visitors to empathize with her story, fostering a deeper understanding and appreciation of her life and work. Her story is a testament to the power of one individual to make a lasting impact, inspiring visitors to consider their potential to shape the world around them.

Historic Preservation

The story of the Molly Brown House is not just about a building but about the power of community involvement in preserving history. In the 1970s, this beautiful building was nearly demolished, and its fate was uncertain. Fortunately, Historic Denver, Inc. intervened with the help of a group of passionate citizens who saved the mansion from destruction. Restoring the home to its former glory was a massive undertaking that required much patience, dedication, and meticulous research. Historians pored over archives to uncover historical documents. At the same time, preservationists searched antique stores and auctions for authentic furnishings and artifacts that reflected the grandeur of the Victorian era. This meticulous attention to detail was not just about creating a visually stunning space but about recreating an atmosphere that would have been familiar to Molly Brown herself. Thanks to this unwavering commitment to preservation, visitors to the Molly Brown House can step back in time and experience Denver's opulence, complexity, and cultural richness in the early 1900s. Through this immersive experience, the Molly Brown House tells the story of Denver's architectural history. It brings to life the societal norms and artistic sensibilities of a bygone era. The preservation efforts of the Molly Brown House Museum are a testament to the importance of preserving our historical heritage, and visitors can feel a sense of gratitude and respect for this work, inspiring them to consider their role in preserving history.

Cultural Programming

The Molly Brown House Museum in Denver offers a wealth of interactive educational programs and events illuminating significant events, women's history, and the importance of preservation efforts. It also provides a unique opportunity for visitors to engage with history actively. Visitors

can partake in Victorian-era Christmas celebrations, which not only showcase the era's traditions but also provide a vivid reminder of the social customs of the time. These festivities are adorned with period-appropriate decor and guided by historical accuracy, offering a unique glimpse into the past's holiday spirit. Additionally, the museum hosts engaging lectures, interactive workshops on Victorian-era crafts, and guided tours that delve into the socio-political climate of Molly Brown's time, providing attendees with a deeper understanding of the challenges and triumphs of Denver's early 20th-century society. By serving as a dynamic center for cultural education, the museum effectively connects historical knowledge with contemporary insights, fostering a community that values the complex history of Denver. A visit to the Molly Brown House Museum is not just a tour but a journey of enlightenment, offering a unique opportunity to actively engage with history meaningfully.

Architectural Jewel

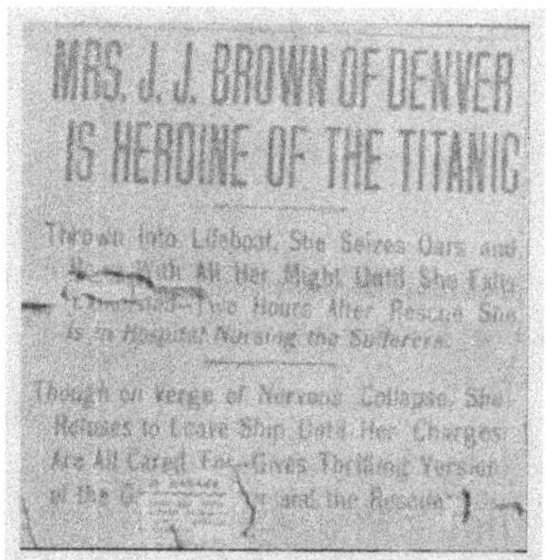

The Molly Brown House is not just a historical landmark; it's a living testament to architectural history. Its unique blend of Queen Anne and Richardsonian Romanesque styles, characterized by their ornate details and steep roofs, intricate woodwork, stained glass, and original furnishings, provide a tangible link to the evolution of Denver's architecture. The house's features are a testament to the city's architectural ambition.

For those planning a visit, a walk through the museum on a crisp autumn afternoon is not just a historical lesson but an immersive journey into Denver's past. Visitors can stand in the same rooms where Molly Brown made decisions that would shape her city, walk on the same floors, and touch the same banisters. The museum's unique features, such as the original furnishings and the stunning stained glass windows, create a palpable link to the history that continues to shape Denver today. The Molly Brown House Museum offers a unique experience, a chance to step back in time and be a part of Denver's rich history. It's an experience that will leave you with a deeper appreciation for Denver's past and a desire to learn more.

The Molly Brown House Museum is more than a tribute to a Titanic survivor; it significantly represents Denver's historical and cultural heritage. Through its preservation, programming, and architecture, the museum offers a multidimensional exploration of Denver's history, inviting visitors to understand the city not only as it is today but as it was in the past. The museum's role in preserving Denver's history is crucial. It serves as a guardian of the city's past, ensuring that future generations can learn from and be inspired by its rich history. Visitors contribute to preserving and celebrating Denver's heritage by supporting the museum. It is a testament to the city's rich past and ongoing commitment to preserving and celebrating its heritage.

FIVE POINTS: JAZZ AND THE HARLEM OF THE WEST

Nestled at the bustling crossroads of Denver, Five Points is not just a neighborhood but a living, breathing entity that vibrates with cultural and historical significance. Its narrative is interwoven with the melodious strains

of jazz that once reverberated through its streets, painting a vivid picture of its past. For instance, did you know that the iconic performance of Duke Ellington at the **Rossonian Hotel** in 1936 drew a diverse audience and marked a pivotal moment in the neighborhood's history? Recognized as the Harlem of the West, Five Points was a hotbed of musical innovation, where iconic figures like Billie Holiday and Duke Ellington left an indelible imprint on the neighborhood and the music industry. The spirit of improvisation was not confined to music but also permeated the community's resilience and creativity, creating a vibrant and dynamic atmosphere. Similarly, Capitol Hill, with its architectural grandeur dating back to the Gilded Age, was the residence of Denver's early elite, who played a significant role in shaping the city's future.

Five Points is not just a neighborhood; it's a testament to resilience. Despite the challenges of segregation, it emerged as a beacon of African American culture and heritage. This cultural renaissance was not limited to music; it sparked a fusion of art, literature, and social activism that defined the community. For instance, the neighborhood's diversity, influenced by African American, European, and Hispanic cultures, is a source of strength and inspiration. This unique blend of cultures, where jazz music coexisted with European art and Hispanic literature, is not just a reflection of the neighborhood's history but also a symbol of its strength and determination.

Five Points is a treasure trove of historical landmarks that bear witness to its rich history and cultural legacy. The Rossonian Hotel, a crown jewel of the neighborhood, stands as a monument to the golden age of jazz. **The Black American West Museum,** not far from the Rossonian, plays a crucial role in preserving the heritage of African American pioneers. The Colorado State Capitol Building, with its stunning architecture and rich history, is a testament to the state's political power and cultural heritage. Did you know the building's golden dome, covered in genuine gold leaf, symbolizes the state's wealth and prosperity? The interior of the building is equally impressive, with its grand staircase, stained glass windows, and murals depicting the state's history.

Five Points' identity is not just a dynamic tapestry but a source of pride and unity, maintaining its character amidst the ebbs and flows of time. This endurance is a testament to the neighborhood's deep-rooted sense of community and unbreakable spirit. Five Points has always been more than just a geographic location; it is a living, breathing entity, a mosaic of stories, dreams, and struggles. The community's pride in its heritage is palpable and infectious, manifesting in festivals, parades, and gatherings celebrating the neighborhood's history and cultural contributions. These events, such as the annual Jazz Festival and the Juneteenth Parade, are not just celebrations but opportunities for the community to come together, share their stories, and strengthen their bonds, fostering a sense of belonging and unity. The active participation of the community in these events and the preservation of the neighborhood's history and culture is a testament to their commitment and love for Five Points. Their efforts in preserving historical landmarks, such as the Rossonian Hotel and the

Black American West Museum, exemplify their dedication to their heritage.

Five Points offers a unique lens through which to view Denver's evolution. Its heartbeat is found in the syncopated rhythms of jazz, the spirited debates of social activists, and the creative expressions of artists and writers. It is a place where history is not confined to textbooks but is lived and breathed. This constant presence shapes the community's identity and aspirations.

As Five Points continues to evolve, its roots remain firmly planted in the rich soil of its history and culture. The legacy of the Harlem of the West endures, speaking of resilience in the face of adversity, community in the face of segregation, and creativity in the face of challenges. In the story of Five Points, Denver finds not just a chapter of its past but also a continuous thread of its cultural and social fabric that weaves through the city's identity, enriching it with every twist and turn. This legacy is a product of the past and a living testament to the community's ongoing efforts to preserve and celebrate its history and culture. The same can be said for Capitol Hill and the Colorado State Capitol Building, where the community's dedication to protecting these historical and cultural landmarks is a shining example of their commitment to their heritage.

CAPITOL HILL: MANSIONS AND HISTORIES

Capitol Hill is an area of Denver that boasts architectural grandeur dating back to the Gilded Age. The streets are lined with buildings that tell stories of ambition, opulence, and the social dynamics that shaped Denver's early days. These buildings, ranging from Victorian to Art Deco, were once the mansions of the city's early elite, who significantly shaped Denver's future. For instance, the Victorian-style mansions, with their ornate facades and intricate detailing, are a testament to the wealth and influence of their former owners. At the same time, the Art Deco buildings reflect the modernist trends of the early 20th century. Each building has a unique history and architectural features, contributing to the rich tapestry of Capitol Hill's past.

Efforts to preserve Capitol Hill's historical essence are not just underway; they are a testament to the community's dedication. Maintaining the character and integrity of the historic district amidst the relentless tide of modern development is a delicate balancing act. Preservationists and historians work tirelessly, often in the face of encroaching urbanization, to safeguard these testaments to Denver's past. Their work, which involves meticulous restoration and innovative adaptation, ensures that the soul of Capitol Hill remains intact, preserving the district's cultural narrative for future generations. These ongoing efforts are a call to action, inviting residents and visitors alike to join in preserving and celebrating Denver's rich history and culture. Whether volunteering, attending preservation events, or simply spreading the word, everyone can play a part in safeguarding Denver's historical and cultural landmarks.

Capitol Hill's transformation from the residential enclave of Denver's affluent to a diverse, vibrant community is a thrilling journey that symbolizes the city's progress towards inclusivity and growth. The district is a blend of old and new, where historic mansions coexist with modern apartments, and  its air resonates with the eclectic sounds of a community that has embraced change. This evolution is evident in the transformation of the Molly Brown House, once the residence of a wealthy socialite, into a museum that celebrates the life and times of Margaret Brown, a prominent social activist. This shift in focus reflects the changing values and priorities of the community, highlighting its resilience and ability to adapt and thrive amid shifting social landscapes. The community's efforts to maintain the district's historic character amidst the changing times are also worth noting.

The narrative of Capitol Hill is a tale of ambition, resilience, and transformation of a city that respects its past while boldly stepping into its future. The district serves as a living museum, a testament to the enduring legacy of those who shaped Denver's early days, and a beacon for those who continue to mold its destiny. In Capitol Hill, the past and present of Denver merge, offering a multifaceted portrait of a city that is forever evolving and reaching new horizons.

THE DENVER CAPITOL BUILDING: A GOLDEN DOME

Symbol of Colorado

The Colorado State Capitol Building is a remarkable architectural feat and a symbol of Colorado's rich history and governance. Its golden dome shines bright, representing the state's unique identity as the "Mile High City." The thirteenth step on the Capitol's western entrance marks precisely one mile above sea level, linking Colorado's character with its geographic landscape. Beyond the legislative proceedings inside, the Capitol stands as a beacon of light, reminding the people of Colorado of their state's evolution from a mining community to a center of innovation and cultural dynamism. The Capitol is crucial to Denver's essence and holds great cultural and historical importance. Visitors can learn about Denver's journey and see examples of historical conservation. The Capitol is a testament to the dreams and accomplishments of Colorado's citizens, and it offers a comprehensive glimpse into the state's progression.

Architectural Features

The Capitol's architectural grandeur, characterized by its neoclassical style, is aesthetically appealing and has a rich history and purpose. The building's intricate designs, such as the use of Doric columns and pediments crafted from the rare and captivating Colorado Rose Onyx marble, showcase the natural wealth of the state and the skill of its artisans. This unique marble, with its mesmerizing hues and patterns, is a testament to the natural wonders of Colorado. The neoclassical style, with its emphasis on symmetry, proportion, and the use of classical elements, is a striking feature of the Capitol's design. Stepping into the halls of the Capitol is not just a visit; it's a journey through time, a unique and captivating experience that leaves visitors in awe of the grandeur that speaks to the ambitions of early Coloradans. The building serves as a bridge between the past and present, and its architecture is a constant reminder of where the state has been and where it is headed.

Public Tours

Visiting the Capitol is a walk through a building and a journey through history. The dome, adorned with intricate stained glass depicting past governors, offers a breathtaking panoramic view of Denver. This sight is sure to leave visitors in awe. As the cityscape has grown and evolved, the Capitol has remained a guardian, always watching over it. The Capitol is not just a symbol of power but a place for the people. Guided tours, open to all and easily accessible, offer not just insights into the building's history and the workings of the state government but a warm and inviting welcome to the public. The Capitol provides [audio guides in multiple languages], ensuring that all visitors can fully appreciate its history and significance, genuinely earning its reputation as the "people's house."

Landmark Legislation

The Colorado State Capitol Building in Denver is not just a building but a symbol of the state's journey from a rugged frontier to a modern beacon of innovation and culture. Its golden dome, shining against the skyline, is a profound statement in the ongoing conversation between architecture and  time. The halls of the Capitol have witnessed landmark legislation and events that have shaped the state and the nation. For instance, it was here that the first women's suffrage bill was introduced in the late 19th century, a pivotal moment in the fight for gender equality that reverberated across the country and led to the eventual ratification of the 19th Amendment. More recently, the Capitol has been at the forefront of renewable energy policy, reflecting Colorado's commitment to environmental sustainability. Each law passed within its walls is a thread in the state's ever-evolving narrative, a testament to Colorado's role as a pioneer in social, environmental, and economic realms. The Capitol is a testament to the power of democracy and the people's resilience, inspiring all who visit.

LARIMER SQUARE: WHERE DENVER BEGAN

Larimer Square, a distinctive cobblestone pathway nestled in the heart of Denver, is a living testament to the city's modest beginnings. This historic block, the oldest in Denver, is a tapestry of pioneers and gold rushes. In the mid-19th century, General William Larimer Jr. laid the foundation for Denver's commercial and social life, setting the stage for the city's urban development. One such tale is the story of the first general store on Larimer Street, which became a gathering place for the early settlers. Imagine the excitement and anticipation as the settlers flocked to this store, their only source of supplies and news from the outside world. Larimer Square is not just a location; it is the birthplace of Denver's identity, a point of origin from which the city's expansive narrative unfolds. For instance, during the gold rush, Larimer Square was a bustling activity center, with miners and prospectors flocking to the area in search of their fortune.

The transformation of Larimer Square from its nascent state to its bustling district today is a narrative of urban renewal and preservation that mirrors Denver's broader evolution. Despite facing the threat of dilapidation, the Victorian buildings and historic facades of Larimer Square stood firm, a testament to their remarkable resilience. The 1960s brought a pivotal moment for the square, with visionary developers recognizing the inherent value of this historic district. Their efforts to revitalize Larimer Square sparked a renaissance of urban preservation in Denver, turning the area into a vibrant commercial and cultural hub while retaining its historical essence. This successful transformation became a model for other cities grappling with the balance between modernization and historic preservation. With its lively atmosphere and thriving businesses, Larimer Square today is a beacon of successful urban renewal. It demonstrates that historical districts can adapt to contemporary needs without sacrificing their soul. Similarly, Union Station's transformation from a transportation hub to a cultural and social center is a testament to Denver's commitment to preserving its history while embracing the future. The economic impact of these transformations cannot be overstated, with Larimer Square and Union Station contributing significantly to Denver's economic growth and development.

Larimer Square is not just a historical site; it's a vibrant cultural hub that pulsates with the energy of Denver's heritage and contemporary culture. The streets are lined with various restaurants, boutique shops, and entertainment venues, each offering a unique experience. Here, one can indulge in cuisines from around the world, shop for unique artisanal crafts, or enjoy a live performance in an intimate theater setting. The square is not just a site for commerce but also a venue for cultural expression, hosting a variety of events that contribute to the vibrant cultural fabric of Denver. These events, such as the annual Larimer Square Arts Festival and the Union Station Summer Concert Series, set against the backdrop of historic buildings, create a dynamic interplay between tradition and innovation, making Larimer Square a microcosm of Denver's broader cultural evolution. For instance, the Larimer Square Arts Festival showcases the works of local artists and artisans, providing a platform for them to share their creativity with the community.

The architectural diversity of Larimer Square is a treasure trove for enthusiasts of Denver's architectural and urban development. The meticulously restored Victorian buildings, with their ornate facades and intricate ironwork, are proud  testaments to the city's past. Each building has a unique architectural feature, such as the D&F Tower, a miniature replica of Venice's Campanile, which stands tall, a reminder of the square's early aspirations. Nearby, former warehouses have been transformed into chic lofts and offices, their industrial past repurposed for contemporary use. This blend of old and new, preservation and innovation, reflects Denver's respect for its heritage and forward-looking ethos. A walk through Larimer Square is a journey through time, with the architectural diversity serving as a testament to the area's adaptability and resilience. Similarly, Union Station's architecture is a blend of Beaux-Arts and neoclassical styles, with its grand facade and intricate detailing showcasing the city's architectural prowess.

Larimer Square's journey from the cradle of Denver's urban development to a symbol of successful preservation and renewal encapsulates the city's ethos. It is a story of vision and perseverance, of recognizing the value of the past while steering confidently into the future. The square remains not just a physical space but a nexus of Denver's identity, a place where history is not just remembered but actively shapes the present. As the city continues to grow and evolve, Larimer Square reminds us of Denver's roots, a touchstone for understanding how far the city has come and the endless possibilities. Similarly, Union Station, with its ongoing renovations and plans for future expansion, continues to symbolize Denver's progress and a testament to the city's commitment to preserving its heritage while embracing modernity. The future of Larimer Square and Union Station is bright, with plans for further development and preservation that will ensure their continued relevance and contribution to Denver's cultural and economic landscape.

UNION STATION: MORE THAN A TRAIN STATION

Union Station in Denver is an impressive symbol of the city's evolution from a tiny frontier settlement to a thriving urban center. This iconic landmark serves as a transportation hub for travelers and a living archive of Denver's growth, representing the values of community and progress. Beyond its function as a transit point, Union Station is an integral part of Denver's identity, embodying the city's past successes and future aspirations. It tells stories of transformation, perseverance, and advancement, positioning itself as a crucial narrative in Denver's unfolding history.

In its current form, Union Station has been transformed into a bustling cultural and social hub, reflecting Denver's communal ethos. The once bustling corridors have been transformed into the Great Hall, a social space with cafes, boutiques, and restaurants contributing to Denver's culinary and commercial innovation. This metamorphosis has revitalized the station into a venue for public events, markets, and cultural celebrations, attracting locals and tourists alike to share communal experiences. Union Station's open doors welcome all, showcasing Denver's commitment to inclusivity and community engagement. It remains a vibrant testament to the city's dynamic spirit, inviting everyone to be a part of Denver's story.

Historic Transport Hub

At the end of the 19th century, Union Station emerged as a pivotal transportation hub, underscoring Denver's significance as a crucial node in the country's railway system. This development brought unprecedented growth, attracting settlers, miners, and entrepreneurs enticed by the promise  of opportunities in the West. With its intricate Beaux-Arts facade and sprawling platforms, the station became the city's lifeblood, facilitating people's movement and exchanging ideas, cultures, and commerce that would shape Denver's socioeconomic landscape. The tracks that extended from Union Station were more than mere steel routes; they were conduits of change, ushering in prosperity that would firmly establish Denver's position in the annals of American urbanization. Today, Union Station continues to play a vital role in Denver's transportation system, serving as a hub for Amtrak and regional light rail services.

Architectural Revitalization

At the turn of the 21st century, Union Station faced a dilemma due to the rise of modern transportation and the decline of rail travel. However, with its deep-rooted appreciation for history, Denver recognized the significance of this iconic landmark and embarked on a comprehensive revitalization project to restore it. The project was about preserving the station's original structure and reimagining its role in a contemporary urban setting. With the help of architects and planners, the station's architectural integrity was meticulously preserved, including its towering windows and ornate interior details, while incorporating modern elements to cater to the needs of today's society. The outcome is a stunning combination of history and modernity, a unique blend that intrigues and inspires every Denverite and visitor.

MODERN MARVELS: CONTEMPORARY ARCHITECTURE

In the heart of Denver, the city's vibrant energy seamlessly merges the old and new, where the skyline serves as a canvas for architectural creativity and innovation. Consider the Denver Art Museum's Frederic C. Hamilton building, a geometric masterpiece that resembles a titanium flower. Its unique design, angular planes, and captivating use of light and shadow are a testament to the city's architectural progress. Another standout is the **Denver International Airport**, a tent-like structure that draws inspiration from the snow-capped peaks of the Rockies. These buildings, with their impressive facades and futuristic concepts, challenge conventional design boundaries while celebrating the city's natural beauty and urban vibrancy, leaving visitors and residents alike in awe and admiration of their grandeur and beauty.

Cutting-Edge Designs

Denver has embraced contemporary architecture, evident in the buildings that deviate from traditional designs to offer a fresh perspective on urban living. The Frederic C. Hamilton building of the Denver Art Museum is a geometric masterpiece that resembles a titanium flower next to its predecessor's castle-like structure. This building, designed by the renowned architect Daniel Libeskind, features angular planes that capture the light and shadow of Colorado's diverse landscape, creating a visual poetry that speaks to the city's artistic soul. Similarly, the Union Station redevelopment project has revitalized a historic hub and transformed it into a lively mixed-use space. It blends the grandeur of its original facade with modern functionality that caters to the needs of contemporary explorers.

Notable Architects

The architects responsible for Denver's impressive modern buildings are innovative thinkers who see the city as an opportunity for architectural experimentation. When designing the Denver International Airport, Curtis Fentress looked to the snow-capped  peaks of the Rockies for inspiration, resulting in a tent-like structure that has become an icon. This building not only redefines the aesthetics of airports but also enhances functionality with a design that overcomes the challenges of Denver's climate. In contrast, Brad Cloepfil's work on the **Clyfford Still Museum** utilizes a minimalist approach, allowing the art inside to take center stage. His design philosophy emphasizes that architecture can serve as a subtle yet powerful background for human activity, shaping the city's landscape and architectural identity. Their contributions to Denver's architectural landscape, such as the iconic Denver International Airport and the minimalist Clyfford Still Museum, should be appreciated by all.

MIXED-USE DEVELOPMENTS

The trend of mixed-use developments in Denver is not just a design choice but a reflection of a holistic approach to urban design. These developments, such as the innovative **Battery621** and **The Source**, involve coexisting residential, commercial, and cultural spaces. They foster community and connectivity, offering a blueprint for sustainable and inclusive urban growth. For instance, the RiNo Art District has transformed industrial buildings into galleries, studios, and living spaces, bringing new life to the neighborhood while preserving its historical essence. These developments serve as microcosms of Denver's larger urban ecosystem, promoting walkability, reducing commute times, and fostering a sense of community. They are a testament to Denver's commitment to sustainable and inclusive design, and their impact on the city's urban growth, fostering a sense of belonging and appreciation for Denver's urban growth, is undeniable. The benefits of these developments, such as fostering community and reducing commute times, are unquestionable.

PUBLIC SPACES AND PARKS

Denver's architectural renaissance centers on creating public spaces and parks that encourage interaction, reflection, and connection. **Civic Center Park**'s redesign embodies this philosophy by balancing open green spaces with civic areas, providing a venue for public discourse and personal tranquility. Similarly, the **South Platte Riverfront** development restores ecology while making it easily accessible, transforming it into a cherished natural refuge that fosters community engagement and outdoor recreation. These spaces are designed with intention and care, highlighting how architecture can enhance the quality of urban life and turn the city into a living, breathing work of art. This innovative and inclusive approach to architecture should inspire us all, igniting a sense of hope and excitement for the bright future of our city's architectural landscape and the quality of urban life it promises.

Contemporary architecture in Denver reflects the city's identity - innovative, inclusive, and deeply connected to its natural surroundings. By embracing mixed-use developments and the bold visions of architects, Denver crafts a narrative of growth that respects its past while looking to the future. The public spaces and parks throughout the city are testaments to Denver's belief in the power of design to foster community, sustainability, and a deeper relationship with the urban environment. In the interplay of light, glass, steel, and greenery, Denver's architectural story unfolds, a tale of a city striving to reach the sky while staying grounded in its rich history and culture. This innovative and inclusive approach to architecture should inspire us all, igniting a sense of hope and excitement for the bright future of our city's architectural landscape.

HISTORIC HOODS: THE ARCHITECTURE OF DENVER'S PAST

Embarking on a journey through Denver's historic neighborhoods, such as Capitol Hill and Highlands, is an exhilarating adventure of discovery. Each brick and beam in these treasure troves of Victorian and Craftsman homes holds a secret, like the hidden passageways used during the Prohibition era in the 1920s. Every ornate doorway whispers a tale of the past. These structures, with their intricate woodwork and majestic facades, are not just remnants of the past but living testaments to the resilience and beauty of their inhabitants.

Preserving Denver's architectural heritage is a testament to the community's unwavering dedication and shared responsibility. Preservation societies and residents unite as caretakers and guardians of these historical landmarks, designating them as beacons of the past. This collective effort shields these structures from the ravages of time, preserving the stories they hold. Capitol Hill and Highlands are vibrant, lived-in spaces, shaping the city's cultural landscape and reminding us of our shared responsibility to protect our heritage.

Architectural tours are a must for a deeper dive into Denver's past. These guided explorations offer a fascinating insight into the architectural styles that define the city's historic districts. They also shed light on the lives of the notable residents who once graced these streets. Each tour is a journey back in time, a chance to witness the evolution of Denver's identity from a frontier town to a bustling metropolis, and a unique opportunity to appreciate the city's rich history.

Denver's approach to adaptive reuse of historic buildings is a testament to its transformative and innovative spirit. Structures like Union Station, once a forgotten railway terminal, have been reborn as bustling transit, dining, and shopping hubs. The adaptive reuse process involves challenges, such as structural issues, zoning regulations, or community resistance, which require careful planning and collaboration. However, the benefits have been immense. The revitalization of Union Station has preserved Denver's history and created a vibrant hub that attracts locals and tourists alike. Similarly, the RiNo district has breathed new life into former industrial buildings, transforming them into galleries, studios, and eateries. These examples of adaptive reuse preserve Denver's history and demonstrate its forward-thinking approach to urban development, sparking our imagination with the possibilities of the future.

Denver's historic neighborhoods are a testament to the city's rich cultural and architectural heritage. Through preservation efforts and adaptive reuse, these neighborhoods continue to tell the story of Denver's past while contributing to its present and future. As we move forward, these areas' enduring beauty and historical significance remind us to cherish and protect our architectural heritage.

FUTURE OF URBAN DEVELOPMENT

Union Station's revitalization is an exemplary model of urban development that showcases the significant impact of heritage-conscious planning on the fabric of a city. Its success has transformed the station and spurred growth and renewal in neighboring areas. For instance, LoDo has seen a surge in new companies and a revitalization of its cultural scene with the opening of new art galleries, theaters, and music venues. This success has set a precedent for future urban projects, demonstrating that historic preservation and urban innovation can coexist and propel communities forward in a symbiotic relationship.

Union Station represents Denver's past, present, and future essence. It is more than just a building or a point on a map; it embodies the spirit of transformation that defines the city. Union Station is a steadfast reminder of where the city has been and where it is going. It symbolizes community, history, and progress as Denver continues to evolve.

As we close this chapter, we are reminded of the enduring legacy of places like Union Station. They are anchors in the swiftly changing currents of time, grounding us in our shared past while guiding us toward a collective future. Denver's story, much like the trains that once defined Union Station, is an ongoing journey, with each chapter building upon the last and moving towards new horizons yet to be discovered. As we turn the page, let us carry forward the lessons of resilience, community, and innovation that these historical landmarks teach us, applying them to the new adventures that await in the coming chapters.

OUTDOOR ADVENTURE ESCAPES

Amidst the vibrant urban landscape of Denver, the call of the wild echoes, serving as a constant reminder of the awe-inspiring natural beauty that envelops the city. The contrast between the majestic mountains and the bustling concrete jungles invites an exploration of the harmonious coexistence of human achievement and natural wonder. This chapter will delve into places where nature's beauty unfolds in a symphony of experiences, each note resonating with the inner adventurer. Among these natural stages, Red Rocks Park and Amphitheatre stand out. Its unique red sandstone formations and natural acoustics create an unparalleled experience, making it a must-visit for any outdoor enthusiast or music lover. Imagine the thrill of a live concert, the sound waves reverberating off the ancient rocks, and the breathtaking view of the city skyline in the distance. This unique experience, where nature and music harmonize, awaits you at Red Rocks Park and Amphitheatre, promising an adventure you won't want to miss.

RED ROCKS PARK: NATURE'S CONCERT HALL

Unique Natural Acoustics

Imagine when the first sound waves reverberated from the angled facades of Ship Rock and Creation Rock, blending in a symphony of perfect

harmony at the heart of the amphitheater. This acoustic wonder is not a coincidence but a geological marvel that took thousands of years to form. Created by the same tectonic forces that shaped the Rocky Mountains, the amphitheater's red sandstone formations create an unmatched natural soundstage. This unique setting allows the ancient rocks to embrace every plucked string, resonant chord, and whispered lyric, producing a sound purity that surpasses the ordinary concert experience. Performers and audiences alike describe a transcendent essence to the music played here, where the natural acoustics elevate live performances to a profound, almost spiritual level. This exceptional phenomenon ensures that every note resonates not only through the space but also through the souls of those present, creating an unforgettable connection with the music that inspires and uplifts.

Hiking and Biking

Red Rocks Park, a sprawling 738-acre playground, extends far beyond the amphitheater, inviting outdoor enthusiasts to embark on a thrilling adventure. The landscape is a vibrant outpouring of trails, each offering a unique and exciting journey. The park caters to all adventure levels, from strolls beneath towering monoliths to challenging bike trails that push even the most experienced cyclists. As you traverse these trails, you'll be rewarded with awe-inspiring views of the Denver skyline and the vast plains that stretch into the horizon. This view, where the urban and natural worlds seamlessly blend, reminds us of the delicate balance we must maintain. Amidst the red rocks, the city's pulse feels distant and familiar, a testament to the worlds we build and the natural world that has always existed.

Sunrise and Yoga

As the sun rises and the sky turns fiery gold, the amphitheater transforms into a serene sanctuary for those seeking tranquility. Yoga at Red Rocks is more than just a physical exercise; it's a communion with the elements.

The solid ground beneath, the open sky above, and the ancient rocks embracing the space create a setting for meditation and rejuvenation that is hard to find elsewhere. This blending of physical wellness and spiritual nourishment under the open sky as the city below awakens offers a sense of clarity and peace in the unrelenting march of time.

It's a moment of pure serenity, a pause in the chaos of life, and a chance to reconnect with yourself and the world around you.

Cultural Significance

Red Rocks Amphitheater is a significant venue in American music history and a revered pilgrimage site for artists and fans. Its allure extends beyond its remarkable natural acoustics. It is deeply imprinted in the collective memory of iconic concerts that transcended mere performances into communal spiritual experiences. These events, where the harmony of music and nature profoundly reminded us of our interconnected humanity, continue to resonate. The amphitheater whispers these historical echoes in the quiet moments between live shows. It is a powerful testament to its role as a performance venue and a sacred space of communal memory. Here, art and nature merge in a unique symbiosis, underscoring Red Rocks' status as a consecrated site where the legacy of musical legends and the timeless beauty of the natural world merge.

Historical Significance

The amphitheater has been designated a National Historic Landmark and is listed on the National Register of Historic Places. The Geological Society of America has also named it one of the Seven Wonders of the Geologic World. The park surrounding the amphitheater contains over 70 species of mammals and over 200 species of birds, making it a popular destination for wildlife enthusiasts.

CONFLUENCE PARK: WHERE WATER AND CITY MEET

Confluence Park is a beautiful sanctuary in the heart of Denver, where the natural and urban elements blend seamlessly. The park is situated at the point where the Platte River and Cherry Creek meet and is symbolic of Denver's origins. Early settlers recognized the land's potential amidst the arid landscape of the American West, and this spot represents the birthplace of Denver. The confluence of the two rivers has become an ongoing story of growth and renewal, reflecting Denver's resilience and unbreakable bond with nature.

Confluence Park, a haven of adventure and tranquility, offers diverse activities to cater to every interest. Whether you're a water sports enthusiast, a cycling lover, or simply someone who enjoys a stroll in nature, Confluence Park has something to offer. From kayaking and paddle-boarding to cycling and leisurely walks, the park promises a day filled with excitement and exploration.

Efforts to restore and maintain the natural habitats within Confluence Park have transformed the area into a beacon of urban ecology. These initiatives, aimed at revitalizing the native flora and fauna, have seen the banks of the Platte River and Cherry Creek come alive with the buzz of pollinators and the rustle of greenery, creating a vibrant contrast to the concrete confines of the city. These restoration projects are about preserving the park's natural beauty and educating the public on the importance of ecological stewardship. By visiting Confluence Park, you're enjoying its beauty and playing a crucial role in its preservation.

Confluence Park, a significant environmental contributor, has evolved into a vibrant community space that fosters strong connections among Denver's diverse populace. The park, with its inviting green spaces and tranquil water bodies, offers a welcoming respite from bustling city life. It hosts a plethora of events, festivals, and public gatherings that draw crowds from the city and beyond, creating a sense of shared experience and community. The park serves as a venue for events and a crucible for community bonding, where shared experiences forge lasting connections among its inhabitants.

Confluence Park symbolizes harmony in the interplay of water and city, where nature's tranquility and urban vitality coexist. It encourages a dialogue between the city and the environment, advocating for a future where such relationships are preserved and nurtured. As the waters of the Platte River and Cherry Creek continue to flow, they carry the stories of a city that has grown alongside them, which finds its reflection in the ebb and flow of their currents. Confluence Park's quiet majesty remains a testament to Denver's origins, present, and unwavering commitment to a future where the natural and the built environment thrive.

DENVER'S BEST HIKING TRAILS FOR EVERY LEVEL

In Denver, hiking trails are woven throughout the natural landscape, offering a variety of experiences for hikers of all levels. From gentle foothills to rugged mountain peaks, each trail tells its own story of geology, history, and the wild spirit of nature.

For families, there are plenty of safe and enjoyable trails to explore, such as the **Bear Creek Trail**, which follows alongside a creek and features interactive nature centers and wildlife sightings. These hikes provide a chance to connect with the natural world and instill a love for the environment in young explorers. For those seeking a more challenging adventure, trails like **Mount Falcon** and **Lookout Mountain** offer awe-inspiring views of the Continental Divide and Denver's iconic skyline. These scenic overlooks, with their breathtaking vistas, serve as a testament to the beauty and grandeur of the wilderness, inspiring hikers with a sense of wonder and deep appreciation for the natural world.

While Denver's trails offer a gateway to nature's wonders, it's crucial to remember that this privilege comes with a responsibility. Trail etiquette, such as staying on the path, leaving no trace, and respecting wildlife, is not just a suggestion but an essential part of preserving the sanctity of these spaces for future generations. By following these guidelines, you're not just ensuring the safety of the trails but also contributing to the preservation of the natural environment.

Denver's trails are more than just paths through the landscape. They offer a connection to the land and a reminder of the beauty and fragility of our world. They inspire us to explore, discover, and protect the natural world and serve as a reflection of our journey through life.

BIKING DENVER: ROUTES THAT WOW

Denver boasts a unique fusion of urban landscapes and natural beauty, creating a perfect playground for cyclists. Located at the base of the majestic Rocky Mountains, the city offers an exceptional opportunity for cyclists to venture from the bustling city center into the breathtaking natural vistas beyond. This journey is not just a physical route but a life-altering experience that can shift your perspective. As cyclists ride through this diverse terrain, they find  themselves in harmony with the natural world, where each wheel turn brings them closer to the earth's rhythm.

City-to-Nature Routes

The pathways leading cyclists from the busy streets of Denver to the lush wilderness surrounding it serve as a means of escape and exploration. One route, the **Platte River Trail**, originates in the shadow of skyscrapers and winds out of the city, following the river's course. This trail gradually reveals the landscape's transformation, beginning with urban parks adorned with public art and leading to open spaces where the city skyline becomes a distant silhouette against the mountains. Similarly, the **Cherry Creek Trail** offers cyclists a journey that starts amidst the bustle of

downtown and guides them towards serene reservoirs that lie like hidden gems on the city's edge. These routes seamlessly blend urban and natural elements, encapsulating Denver's unique charm and offering cyclists an experience that nourishes the soul and challenges the body. The transition from the city to the wilderness is a sight to behold, and the serene reservoirs offer a peaceful retreat from the urban hustle.

Bike-Friendly City

Thanks to a series of initiatives promoting a bike-friendly culture, Denver has become a cyclist-friendly haven. As a result of these efforts, the city's infrastructure boasts an extensive network of bike lanes that provide safe passage through busy streets and quiet neighborhoods and instill a sense of security in every cyclist. Additionally, shared bike programs are available throughout the city, with stations that reflect the community's embrace of cycling as a sustainable mode of transport. Denver's vision for a cyclist-safe city includes continuous improvements to existing routes and expanding bike lanes, ensuring that cyclists of all ages and skill levels can traverse the city confidently and efficiently. These efforts, supported by policy and community advocacy, demonstrate Denver's dedication to creating a space where cycling can be freely enjoyed. This commitment is not just about infrastructure; it's about fostering a sense of community. This is evident in the many bikes trailing Denver's daily paths, each a testament to our city's shared love for cycling.

If you are interested in renting a bike in Denver, there are a few options. The first option is to rent a bike from a local bike shop. Some popular bike rental shops in Denver include **B-Cycle**, **Denver Bike Rentals**, and **BikeSource**. These rental shops offer a variety of bike types, including road bikes, mountain bikes, and electric bikes, at affordable rates. You can check their websites for pricing and availability.

Another option is to use Denver's bike-sharing program, B-Cycle. To use B-Cycle, you can download the B-Cycle app or visit one of the many bike stations located throughout the city. Once registered and paid for your rental, you can check out a bike from any station and ride it around the city. The first 30 minutes of your ride are free; after that, there is a small fee for each additional 30 minutes. B-Cycle bikes are designed for short trips and are ideal for visitors who want to explore the city's bike lanes and trails.

Whether you rent a bike in Denver, it's a great way to get around and experience the city's bike-friendly culture. Just follow all traffic laws and wear a helmet for your safety.

Mountain Biking Trails

For those seeking a thrilling adventure beyond the city, Denver's mountain biking trails offer an exhilarating escape. Imagine the rush of wind as you speed down a forest trail, the scent of pine filling the air. **Apex Park**, a paradise for mountain bikers, is just one of the many thrilling destinations. Its trails wind through forests and over ridges, each turn a new chapter in a story of earth and sky. The bike becomes more than just a mode of transport but a partner in a dance of speed and agility, where every rock and root are steps in a choreography dictated by the mountain's ancient rhythms. The thrill of conquering these trails is only matched by the camaraderie of fellow riders, united in the pursuit of pushing limits and capturing moments of triumph amidst the wild. It's an adventure waiting to be experienced, a thrill that can't be put into words, and a journey that will leave you craving more.

Cycling Events

Denver's cycling community is a vibrant and inclusive one, hosting a wide range of events throughout the year. From casual social rides to competitive races, there's something for everyone. **The Denver Century Ride** is a shining example of an event that embodies the joy of cycling. These events are not just for the elite or the experienced but for everyone. They celebrate individual achievements while fostering a shared passion that brings together people of all ages, backgrounds, and skill levels. During these rides, the streets and trails become a symbol of solidarity where the only competition is the inner voice that pushes cyclists to go further, climb higher, and achieve more. It's a community that welcomes and encourages everyone to join, to challenge themselves, and to experience the joy of cycling.

In addition to the Denver Century Ride, Denver's cycling calendar is filled with a variety of engaging biking events. **The Tour de Fat** remains a highlight, offering a delightful mix of biking, beer, and live music courtesy of the New Belgium Brewing Company. For mountain biking enthusiasts, the **Pikes Peak APEX** presents a challenging multi-day race on the slopes of America's Mountain, with options to participate for one, two, or all three days. The **Go Pro Mountain Games** feature road and mountain bike races in the scenic town of Vail. For those looking to contribute to a noble cause, the **Ride to End ALZ** is a fully-supported fundraising ride ranging from 10 to 75 miles supporting Alzheimer's research. These events cater to cyclists of varying skill levels and offer a chance to experience the camaraderie and joy of biking across Denver's diverse landscapes.

Cycling in Denver is more than just a way to get around; it's a way to explore the city's unique blend of urban and natural environments. The city's numerous paths and trails allow cyclists to journey from the city's heart, bustling streets, and vibrant neighborhoods into the surrounding natural beauty, with its serene parks and scenic mountain views. Denver's identity as a city united by a love of cycling is apparent in the colorful mosaic of exploration, fellowship, and a shared yearning for what lies ahead. It's an invitation to all seeking kinship on life's journey, one pedal at a time.

THE BOTANICAL GARDENS: A KALEIDOSCOPE OF COLORS

The Denver Botanic Gardens is a unique and captivating attraction in the heart of Denver. It spans over 24 acres and is a living museum showcasing a diverse collection of plants from around the world, including various rare and endangered species.

The Mordecai Children's Garden, a favorite among families, offers many hands-on activities for kids to learn about the natural world in a fun and interactive way. The gardens also feature a Japanese Garden, a Rock Alpine Garden, and a Boettcher Memorial Tropical Conservatory, home to various exotic plants and flowers.

Throughout the year, the gardens host a variety of events and exhibitions, including concerts, art shows, and plant sales. And if you're a foodie, check out the Offshoots Café, which serves delicious and healthy fare made from fresh, locally sourced ingredients.

Whether you're a nature enthusiast, an art lover, or just looking for a peaceful escape from the city, the Denver Botanic Gardens is a must-visit destination that offers something for everyone.

GREEN SPACES IN THE CITY: DENVER'S URBAN PARKS

Amidst the bustling cityscape of Denver, there are pockets of greenery that beckon, offering a serene escape. These parks, scattered like precious gems throughout the city, are the lungs of Denver, breathing life into the concrete jungle. They are tranquil guardians, providing residents and tourists a sanctuary to reconnect with nature, a rare and precious commodity in the sprawling metropolis.

Denver's parks are not mere green spaces but unique stages where the daily drama of city life unfolds. Children's laughter and the rhythmic sound of joggers and runners blend in, creating a vibrant symphony. These parks also offer sports facilities, allowing competitive spirits to chase victory under the open sky. Each park has unique features, from the stunning views of the Rocky Mountains at Red Rocks Park to the serene lakes at Washington Park, catering to Denver's people's diverse needs and passions.

The roots of Denver's urban parks run deep into the city's history. They were not just created as afterthoughts but as deliberate acts, acknowledging the need for nature amidst the concrete jungle. Places like City Park's vast lawns and winding pathways were designed to contrast the urban sprawl, creating peaceful oases in the expanding city. These parks, each carrying a unique story of its creation, a design that reflects its time, and a distinctive contribution to the city's diverse urban landscape, have gradually become part of Denver's fabric. They are living testaments to the city's past, present, and future.

City Park Jazz in the Park, an iconic summer event that draws in thousands of residents and visitors, is a unique blend of jazz music, community spirit, and beautiful surroundings. Held every Sunday evening from June to August, this free event features a rotating lineup of musicians and bands, playing everything from classic jazz to contemporary fusion. It's a family-friendly event, with kids' activities and food trucks adding to the festive feel.

The event features a rotating lineup of musicians and bands, playing everything from classic jazz to contemporary fusion. Attendees are encouraged to bring blankets, chairs, and picnic baskets, creating a relaxed and welcoming atmosphere. The event is family-friendly, with kids' activities and food trucks adding to the festive feel.

City Park Jazz in the Park is more than just a music event; it's a celebration of community and togetherness. The event brings people from all walks of life together, creating a shared experience and space. It's a place where people can let their hair down, kick back, and enjoy the beauty of nature and the richness of jazz music.

City Park Jazz in the Park is a testament to Denver's commitment to creating vibrant and inclusive public spaces. It showcases the city's love of music, community, and nature and is a must-visit for anyone looking to experience the best Denver has to offer.

Denver's parks are not just green spaces but sanctuaries for our well-being. They offer more than just physical exercise; they provide a space for relaxation and contemplation, a respite for our minds amidst the hustle and bustle of city life. The psychological benefits of spending time in nature, of stealing moments from the day to sit under a tree or beside a stream, are well-documented, serving as a remedy for the stresses of urban living. These green spaces are where our city breathes, finds peace, and rejuvenates.

Denver's parks are more than just green spaces; they are the beating heart of our community. They are the spaces where people from all walks of life come together, where the barriers that divide us fade away under the sun's warmth. Festivals, concerts, community gardens, and farmers' markets unite us, creating bonds and strengthening our social fabric. These events and spaces, crucial to our city's core, are not just for entertainment or sustenance but for building connections and creating a  sense of belonging and shared responsibility. They are the heart of our community, beating with the rhythm of shared experiences and spaces.

As the chapter on Denver's green spaces ends, it leaves behind the echoes of footsteps on paths covered in leaves, memories of laughter under vast open skies, and gentle reminders of nature's enduring presence in the urban landscape. These parks, with their numerous activities, rich history, and contributions to community and wellness, stand as testaments to Denver's commitment to a life where the urban and the natural coexist. They remind us that even in the city's heart, we can still feel the earth's heartbeat, a rhythm that guides, heals, and connects us to something greater.

In Denver's grand narrative, these green spaces are vital chapters in the story of growth, resilience, and community that intertwine with the broader story of the city. As we look to the future, let us carry the lessons learned under the canopy of trees and the vast expanse of the sky, a reminder of the balance that sustains us, the beauty that surrounds us, and the community that unites us.

FAMILY FUN AND KID-FRIENDLY ADVENTURES

Denver, a city brimming with family-friendly excitement, offers a unique blend of cultural richness, educational opportunities, and recreational activities. The Denver Zoo, a standout among these attractions, captivates families with its distinctive blend of immersive nature experiences and educational enrichment. In this chapter, we'll guide you through the zoo's lush pathways, each exhibit a testament to wildlife conservation, educational enrichment, and the joy of family moments amidst nature's marvels. From the awe-inspiring grandeur of the African savannah to the intriguing realm of reptiles, the zoo caters to all interests, making it a must-visit for families with children.

THE DENVER ZOO: A WILD FAMILY DAY OUT

Animal Exhibits

The Denver Zoo is a thrilling adventure, a miniature version of the Earth's diverse ecosystems. It offers a unique opportunity to observe species from around the world. When you're there, you'll hear the roar of a lion, as primal as the savannahs of Africa, where it comes from. The Tropical

Discovery exhibit is a humid haven under a glass dome, abundant with vibrant colors and sounds of the rainforest. Emerald boas coil languidly on branches, and dart frogs hop amidst the foliage. Imagine strolling through Predator Ridge, where the line between observer and observed blurs. You'll have encounters with big cats that are educational and heart-pounding. Each habitat in the zoo is curated carefully to mimic natural environments. They showcase the beauty and diversity of wildlife and serve as a living classroom where families can learn about the delicate balance of ecosystems and the importance of each species within them. It's a place where the wonders of nature come alive, sparking curiosity and empathy in the hearts of all who walk its paths.

Conservation Efforts

The Denver Zoo, a renowned institution and leader in conservation, is a living testament to the sustainable coexistence of humans and nature. The zoo spearheads various global initiatives, including breeding programs to bolster endangered species populations and habitat preservation projects to safeguard wildlife in their natural environments. These conservation efforts are not just behind the scenes; they are shared with the public through educational exhibits and talks. A visit to the zoo is more than a fun outing; it's an opportunity to join the conservation movement by making changes in our daily lives that promote a healthier planet, making it a perfect destination for families interested in both fun and education.

Family Activities

The zoo offers a wealth of opportunities for families to explore the animal kingdom together. Interactive feeding sessions allow children to engage with giraffes, creating a moment of connection that sparks curiosity and excitement. The zoo's educational programs, tailored for different age groups, engage young minds in zoology through behind-the-scenes tours and hands-on animal care experiences. These programs entertain and foster empathy and responsibility towards wildlife, inspiring the next generation of conservationists.

Sustainable Practices

The Denver Zoo is committed to sustainability and implements eco-friendly practices. From waste reduction and recycling initiatives to using renewable energy sources such as solar panels, the zoo ensures that it has a minimal impact on Denver's resources. This dedication to conservation is an essential part of the zoo's identity, and it shares its sustainability story with visitors, proving that even institutions that house a diverse range of wildlife can operate sustainably.

Situated in the heart of Denver, the zoo is more than just an attraction. It's a microcosm of the world's wild beauty, a hub of education, conservation, and family bonding. Visitors can experience the wonders of nature and learn about the importance of empathy and connection. The Denver Zoo is an invitation to listen, learn, and protect the environment. Families can embark on a journey beyond just observing animals; they can step into a story of shared responsibility for our planet's future.

Here, in the vibrant and varied exhibits of the Denver Zoo, the wild heart of the world beats, calling us all to come and experience the beauty of nature.

CHILDREN'S MUSEUM OF DENVER: LEARNING MADE FUN

The Children's Museum is not just a place of fun but a treasure trove of interactive knowledge. It's a space that encourages children and their guardians to explore and discover new things imaginatively and educationally. Every corner and corridor is designed to inspire wonder and promote learning. The museum offers an interactive experience where children can use their senses to explore new ideas and concepts. It's a space that invites children to actively participate in their learning journey, where they can discover and learn through play and exploration, making learning a fun and engaging experience.

Interactive Exhibits

The Children's Museum is not just a place to look but to touch, manipulate, and engage directly with the materials and concepts presented. In the Art Studio, children can explore the magic of color, texture, and form, creating stories on blank canvases with their fingers. At the Energy Exhibit, they can transform into engineers of their miniature worlds, exploring the forces that power our lives. These environments, rich in stimuli and free from the fear of 'doing it wrong,' are fertile grounds for critical thinking and creativity, nurturing seeds of future innovation and artistic expression. It's a fun and interactive space where learning is easy, sparking curiosity and imagination.

Educational Programs

The museum's exhibits are undeniably fascinating, but its value lies in its dedication to education. The calendar is filled with workshops and events, each providing a chance for deeper engagement with topics ranging from astronomy to zoology. Led by enthusiastic educators, these programs are not just simple lessons but exciting learning experiences designed to cater to the different developmental stages of children. Storytimes bring tales from far-off places to life, cultivating a love for reading. At the same time, science workshops help to explain the wonders of the physical world, transforming abstract concepts into tangible experiences. For families, these programs create a shared space for growth, where the pleasure of learning becomes a collective endeavor.

Family Engagement

The Children's Museum in Denver is a one-of-a-kind space that sparks wonder and joy through play. Its innovative design, characterized by open spaces and interactive zones, is a testament to its uniqueness. The exhibits, far from being isolated, form a network of landscapes that invite families to embark on a journey of exploration and discovery together. In the Bubble Room, parents and children can witness the enchanting spectacle of

soap and water, creating ethereal bubbles that float with the weightlessness of dreams. The magic of these moments is two-fold: capturing the essence of wonder and fostering a sense of togetherness. These interactions, filled with laughter and shared amazement, underscore the museum's dual role as an educational institution and a place that strengthens family bonds.

Accessibility and Inclusivity

The Children's Museum in Denver is a shining example of inclusivity and accessibility, ensuring that all children, regardless of their abilities or backgrounds, can fully participate in the learning and exploration experience. The museum's commitment to inclusivity is evident in its provision of ramps, tactile guides, and sensory-friendly hours to ensure every child can enjoy the exhibits. Moreover, the museum's scholarships and community outreach initiatives are a testament to its dedication to removing financial barriers to access. The museum recognizes the transformative power of education and play, valuing each child's unique perspective as a valuable contribution to the diverse tapestry of exploration that the museum fosters. The Children's Museum is not just a place of learning but a beacon of hope and opportunity, inviting all children to embark on a joyful journey of discovery.

ELITCH GARDENS: THRILLS AND SPILLS IN THE CITY

Located within Denver's urban landscape is the exhilarating Elitch Gardens, where leisure and excitement combine to offer a diverse range of attractions that cater to all ages and preferences. As Denver's leading family-oriented amusement and water park, Elitch Gardens sprawls over acres of land, each corner brimming with exciting features that will get the pulse racing and create lifelong memories. From the towering roller coasters that dominate the skyline to the refreshing waves of the water park, visitors are guaranteed a panorama of entertainment and fun.

The story of Elitch Gardens is a captivating journey through time, a testament to its rich history and evolution. Its origins as a zoological park in the late 19th century are a fascinating starting point. Over the years, it has evolved into a vibrant amusement hub, mirroring Denver's growth and dynamism. From its humble beginnings as a garden and cultural center that fostered a connection with nature and the arts, the park has undergone numerous transformations, introducing new experiences and attractions that align with evolving tastes and technological advancements. Today, standing on the grounds of Elitch Gardens, one can feel the legacy of joy and innovation that has been its hallmark for over a century.

Seasonal events at Elitch Gardens infuse the park's already vibrant atmosphere with an extra dose of excitement and charm, perfectly reflecting the spirit of the times. During Halloween, Fright Fest envelops the park in a spine-chilling aura, with ghouls and haunted houses eagerly awaiting the brave.

In contrast, summer concerts bring the park to life with a variety of artists that draw crowds, providing the perfect soundtrack to the memories being created. These events serve as more than attractions-they are bridges, connecting the community through shared experiences and fostering a sense of belonging and collective joy.

Elitch Gardens is committed to providing visitors with an inclusive and safe environment. The park prioritizes safety and accessibility measures, with attractions undergoing daily inspections to ensure they operate within the highest safety standards. Moreover, accessibility is a fundamental aspect of Elitch Gardens' ethos, with the park's layout and attractions designed to cater to guests of all abilities. This unwavering dedication to safety and inclusivity is intrinsic to the park's identity. It reflects its role as a venue for entertainment and a space where families can explore, laugh, and grow together, free from worry.

Elitch Gardens encapsulates Denver's spirit - dynamic, inclusive, and ever-evolving. It is a monument to the joy of shared experiences, the thrill of discovery, and the enduring charm of family adventures. Amidst the whirl of rides and the splash of water, the park weaves tales of connection, creating exhilarating moments that become the threads of shared family lore. Under the vast Colorado sky, Elitch Gardens beats with a rhythm of unabashed joy, inviting all who enter to partake in the dance.

DENVER AQUARIUM: AN UNDERWATER ADVENTURE

The Denver Aquarium stands out as a unique marine life sanctuary in the bustling city of Denver. It offers an unparalleled aquatic adventure, immersing visitors in the diverse habitats of the marine world, from the tranquil currents of Colorado's rivers to the vast depths of the ocean.

The aquarium's vast premises boast meticulously curated exhibits that not only showcase the aquatic wonders of the world but also evoke a profound sense of wonder and awe. Each tank is a window into the diverse habitats that cradle life beneath the water's surface. Visitors can marvel at the trout and basses that dart through the freshwater streams that meander through the landscapes of Colorado. They can also explore the brackish estuaries where rivers meet the sea, which is rich in biodiversity. Here, the mudskipper's curious gaze and the jellyfish's graceful drift invite contemplation on life's adaptability. The journey culminates in the heart of the ocean exhibit, where visitors are enveloped in the vast blue sky and can witness the silent power of sharks and the shimmering beauty of schools of fish.

The exhibits offer captivation and a unique opportunity for deep engagement. They provide insights into the lives of aquatic inhabitants, their roles in their ecosystems, and the delicate balance that sustains them. Interactive experiences abound, from touch tanks where starfish rest in the palm to feeding demonstrations revealing the intricate complexities of aquatic food chains. These interactive moments transform observation into active participation, fostering a deeper bond with the marine world.

The Denver Aquarium is a place of wonder and a hub of education. It skillfully combines knowledge and awe, captivating visitors of all ages. Its regular programs are designed to unravel the mysteries of marine biology, conservation, and oceanography. Workshops  delve into the intricate world of coral reefs and the crucial role of wetlands. These educational initiatives aim to ignite a passion for the marine world, inspiring visitors to protect its beauty and diversity for future generations.

At the core of the Denver Aquarium's mission is conservation. This commitment is evident in every aspect of its operation. The aquarium conducts research programs that delve into the science of marine conservation, exploring sustainable practices to protect endangered species and their habitats. Its efforts extend beyond its walls, actively participating in global initiatives for habitat preservation, species rehabilitation, and mitigating human impacts on the oceans. Public awareness campaigns aim to transform visitors into advocates for the marine environment, with each story underscoring the urgency of the conservation message.

The aquarium is family-friendly, with features that ensure its wonders are accessible to visitors of all ages. The layout invites exploration, with pathways that wind past tanks aglow with the colors of marine life. This leads to interactive zones where curiosity is rewarded with discovery. Special events themed around holidays and marine milestones add excitement to the aquarium experience, transforming it into a place of celebration and learning.

In the interplay of light and shadow, where the water dances with life, the Denver Aquarium offers a sanctuary where the city meets the sea, and the stories of the deep are told in whispers and waves.

DINOSAUR RIDGE: WHERE PREHISTORY COMES ALIVE

Dinosaur Ridge, nestled at the foothills of the majestic Rocky Mountains near Denver, is a site of profound paleontological significance that stirs the curiosity of both the young and the young at heart. Here, the past is

not a distant memory buried in the depths of time. It is a living, breathing entity, exposed under the vast Colorado sky, offering a tangible connection to the ancient creatures that once roamed this land. We assure you of safety measures that ensure a secure and enjoyable visit for all so you can fully immerse yourself in the wonder and awe of this prehistoric world.

Dinosaur Ridge not only offers a visual spectacle, but it is also a place where history is etched into the rocks. Visitors can tread the same ground that dinosaurs once did and explore prehistory. Each fossil and footprint tells a story of a world that has long vanished, of ecosystems that thrived and faltered through the eons. These remnants of the past are not just relics to be observed but keys to understanding the grand narrative of life on Earth, offering insights into the evolution, extinction, and ever-changing dynamics of our planet's biodiversity.

Guided tours at Dinosaur Ridge are not just visual spectacles but enlightening journeys into the past. Led by knowledgeable guides armed with captivating stories and deep insights into the landscape's formation, these tours provide a rich context to visitors. They decode the rocks' language, unveiling the significance of each finding, from the delicate imprint of a leaf to the monumental impression of a Brontosaurus's foot. These tours are not just educational excursions but immersive experiences that bridge the gap between science and imagination, inviting participants to ponder the vast periods and the fleeting nature of existence, leaving them feeling informed and enlightened.

Dinosaur Ridge's educational opportunities are vast and diverse, designed to ignite curiosity and foster a deeper appreciation for science. Our school programs and workshops offer hands-on activities that transform participants into budding paleontologists. Whether your child is in elementary or high school, they can uncover replicas of fossils, learning the meticulous excavation process and the thrill of discovery. By bringing the distant past to life, these programs encourage a sense of wonder and inquiry, laying the foundation for a lifelong engagement with science and the natural world.

At the heart of Dinosaur Ridge's mission lies a deep commitment to conservation and preservation. This site, renowned for its scientific and educational value, is meticulously maintained to ensure that these  prehistoric treasures endure for future generations to explore. Ongoing efforts to shield the site from erosion and the ravages of climate change stand as a testament to the community and scientists' unwavering dedication. Through these conservation initiatives, Dinosaur Ridge is a poignant reminder of the delicate balance between discovery and preservation, a call to action to safeguard our planet's heritage. We invite you to join us in this noble cause, fostering a sense of responsibility and commitment.

Dinosaur Ridge stands as a monument to the awe-inspiring history of our planet, where the past is palpable, and the stories of ancient giants are told in stone. Visitors are invited to contemplate the grandeur of Earth's history and humanity's role within it. This site is a portal to the ancient past and reflects our position in the grand narrative of existence. As we move forward, let us carry with us the lessons of the past, the curiosity to explore, and the commitment to preserve the wonders of our world for the explorers yet to come.

In a city that pulsates with the rhythm of the modern age, places like Dinosaur Ridge offer a rare pause, a moment to look back and marvel at life's journey on our planet. From the silent tales etched in stone to the vibrant narratives of the present, Denver encapsulates the essence of discovery, education, and conservation. As we transition from the echoes of prehistory to the unwritten stories, let us tread lightly, with respect for the past and hope for the future, embracing the adventure that awaits in the coming chapters.

RAINY DAYS IN DENVER

Denver is known for its sunny days, but when the rain starts to fall, there are still plenty of fun activities for families to enjoy. Here are some additional ideas for rainy-day activities in Denver:

- **Denver Museum of Nature and Science:** The Denver Museum of Nature and Science is a great place to spend a rainy day with the family. It features a variety of exhibits on natural history, space exploration, and more, as well as an IMAX theater and planetarium.
- **Denver Art Museum:** The Denver Art Museum is another excellent option for a rainy day. It features a collection of over 70,000 works of art, including paintings, sculptures, and installations.
- **Butterfly Pavilion:** The Butterfly Pavilion is an indoor tropical conservatory home to over 1,600 butterflies. Visitors can walk through the conservatory, see the butterflies up close, and learn about their life cycles and habitat.
- **Denver Public Library:** The Denver Public Library is a great place to spend a rainy day with the family. It features a variety of books, movies, and other resources for all ages, as well as regular programs and events for kids and teens.
- **Denver Escape Room:** The Denver Escape Room is a fun and challenging activity for older kids and teenagers. It's an interactive puzzle game where players are "locked" in a room and must solve clues and riddles to escape.
- **History Colorado Center:** The History Colorado Center is a museum that explores the history of Colorado through interactive exhibits and programs. It's a great place to learn about the state's past, from the Native American tribes who lived here to the pioneers and explorers who helped shape the region.

FOODIE FINDS AND CULINARY GEMS

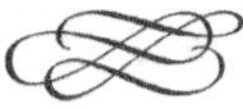

Denver offers a culinary experience that is both diverse and vibrant. This chapter unveils a myriad of dishes that not only tantalize the taste buds but also embody the very essence of Denver's unique dining scene. Each dish is a portal to a narrative of cultural heritage, innovation, and the bountiful terrain of Colorado. From the comforting smothered burrito to the intriguing Rocky Mountain oysters, Denver's culinary offerings are a fusion of history and flavor. As a reader, your role is to immerse yourself in these culinary delights, which have now become integral to Denver's rich culinary narrative.

Denver's food story is not just a collection of recipes but a vibrant tapestry of traditional recipes, playful innovations, and an unwavering commitment to sustainability. The city's iconic dishes are more than just food; they are cultural touchstones that bridge the past and the present. These dishes, steeped in history and flavor, are the soul of Denver's food scene. They invite you to be a part of its vibrant heritage and to understand the city's cultural fabric through its culinary delights.

DENVER'S MUST-TRY DISHES

Iconic Bites

The smothered burrito, a beloved classic, is a testament to the warmth and complexity of Denver's culinary culture. This dish, wrapped in a soft flour tortilla, epitomizes comfort food. At the **Original Chubby's** on 38th Avenue, you can savor the most authentic version of this local favorite. Picture this: a hearty dish with tender chunks of beef or chicken smothered in a spicy green chili sauce and every fold filled with melted cheese. Eating it, you'll experience a perfect combination of spice, texture, and heartiness that will nourish your soul.

Gourmet Bison

Bison, a symbol of the West, is gaining popularity as a healthier alternative to beef and can now be found on many menus in Denver. It's a great example of the trend towards embracing the Old West heritage, as seen at the **Buckhorn Exchange**. The restaurant's walls are adorned with memorabilia and artifacts of the region's past, and the bison steak served there is a prime example of the quality of meat from this iconic animal. The rich flavor of the steak, with its tender and juicy texture, is a testament  to the bison's wild heritage, and eating it is a culinary adventure that speaks to the land. In addition, consuming bison meat is a conscious choice, a nod to sustainable eating practices, and a bridge to Colorado's frontier past.

Rocky Mountain Oysters

For those unfamiliar, Rocky Mountain oysters are a traditional dish that challenges preconceived notions of food and rewards the adventurous. At The Buckhorn Exchange, these deep-fried bull testicles are seasoned and served with a sly smile, a testament to the pioneer spirit and a reminder that culinary boundaries are there to be crossed in Denver. Eating them takes true culinary bravery, involving stepping into the unknown. But it also comes with bragging rights and a unique story, as the dish is a part of Denver's culinary heritage and a symbol of the city's adventurous spirit.

Palisade Peaches

During the warm summer months in Denver, an unmistakable fragrance fills the air—the sweet and succulent aroma of Palisade peaches. These peaches, known to capture the essence of Colorado's abundant sunshine, are highly sought after by locals and tourists alike. Fortunately, the **Denver Farmers Market** is the perfect place to find these juicy and tender fruits, with vendors selling them in abundance from overflowing stalls.

Many of the city's restaurants, such as **The Kitchen Denver**, have also found creative ways to incorporate these peaches into their dishes and desserts. For instance, diners can enjoy a refreshing peach salad sprinkled with local goat cheese or indulge in a warm, delicious cobbler that tastes like a lazy, late-summer afternoon.

These delicious fruits are much more than just a tasty treat - they are also a celebration of local produce and a tribute to the hardworking farmers who nurture the land. In many ways, the Palisade peach has become an iconic symbol of Colorado's verdant countryside and its rich agricultural heritage.

Rocky Ford Cantaloupe

The Rocky Ford Cantaloupe is a highly coveted type of cantaloupe grown in the Arkansas Valley, just a few hours' drive from Denver. This region is known for its fertile soil, irrigated by the Arkansas River, and its unique climate, which gives the fruit its exceptional taste. The fruit is named after the picturesque town of Rocky Ford, located in this agricultural region.

From mid-August through September, Rocky Ford Cantaloupes can be found at local farmers' markets and grocery stores in Denver and surrounding areas. This fruit is a favorite among food enthusiasts and chefs who appreciate its distinctive flavor and versatility. The fruit's succulent and sweet flavor adds a refreshing touch to summer salads and smoothies while bringing elegance to savory dishes like grilled meats or roasted vegetables.

The Rocky Ford Cantaloupe is a true treasure of Colorado. Its unique taste has earned it a reputation as one of the finest cantaloupes in the world. Whether you are a culinary expert or a home cook, this fruit is a must-try when visiting Denver or the surrounding areas.

Olathe Corn

Denver, with its love of good food and fresh produce. It's no wonder that Olathe corn, a widespread variety of sweet corn grown in the state, is a favorite among Denverites.

During the summer months, from late June to early September, Denver locals and visitors can find Olathe corn in local farmer's markets and grocery stores throughout the city and nearby areas. This corn is grown only in a small region in Colorado, located in the Uncompahgre Valley, known for its fertile soil and ideal climate conditions for growing this type of corn. Thanks to its proximity to Denver, residents and visitors can enjoy Olathe corn freshly harvested and delivered to local markets.

The farmers in the Uncompahgre Valley use sustainable and eco-friendly practices to ensure the production of high-quality corn. They harvest the corn by hand when it reaches its peak maturity, ensuring that only the best quality corn makes it to the market. This attention to detail and commitment to quality is evident in Olathe corn's exceptional flavor and tender texture.

Olathe corn can be prepared in various ways. It can be boiled, grilled, or roasted and used as a side dish or added to salads, soups, and many other dishes. Many food enthusiasts in Denver consider Olathe corn a local delicacy and seek it out to experience its unique taste and texture.

THE EVOLUTION OF THE DENVER BRUNCH SCENE

In Denver, brunch has evolved from traditional late-morning fare to a platform for culinary innovation and cultural expression. The meal has transformed into a kaleidoscope of flavors and experiences that mirrors  the city's dynamic spirit. My first brunch experience in Denver was a revelation, with a menu that was a delightful mix of familiar favorites and intriguing new dishes. Each brunch spot offers a unique experience, from the innovative dishes to the vibrant atmosphere, promising to ignite your taste buds and leave you craving more. Whether it's the fusion of Latin American and Asian flavors at **Super Mega Bien** or the elegant take on brunch at **The Bindery**, Denver's brunch scene is a treasure trove of culinary adventures.

The evolution of Denver's brunch scene can be traced back to the early 2000s when a few restaurants embarked on a thrilling culinary adventure with brunch. These pioneers, such as **Snooze, an A.M. Eatery**, challenged the status quo, introducing Denver to a world where pancakes could be canvases for artisanal toppings and Eggs Benedict could be redefined with layers of flavor complexity. With items like Pineapple Upside-Down Pancakes and Habanero Pork Belly Benedicts, Snooze's menu became synonymous with the new brunch wave, a daring departure from the conventional that captivated the palates of Denverites. This innovative approach to brunch has since become a hallmark of Denver's food culture, reflecting the city's spirit of culinary adventure and creativity.

As the brunch scene flourished, it became a battleground for creativity, with each new spot striving to leave its mark through unique dishes, ambiance, and an unwavering commitment to quality. The Bindery, with its sleek, sunlit space overlooking LoHi, offers an elegant take on brunch. Its menu reflects refined tastes and global influences, and the atmosphere is one of relaxed sophistication. Denver's brunch spots, in their diversity, share a common thread -- a desire to elevate the mundane into something memorable, transforming a meal into a moment. Imagine yourself in these spaces, surrounded by the buzz of conversation and the aroma of delicious food, as you embark on a culinary journey.

The trend of bottomless brunches took root in Denver, fostering a strong sense of community and shared experiences. This concept beautifully marries the city's love for craft beverages with the convivial spirit of communal dining. Spots like **ViewHouse Ballpark** and **Linger** embraced this trend, their offerings of endless mimosas and Bloody Marys becoming a staple of weekend gatherings. More than a meal, these brunches are a celebration, a time when friends and families come together to savor not just the food and drink but the joy of shared experiences. The popularity of bottomless brunches speaks to Denver's ethos of generosity and abundance, where good food, good drinks, and good company are seen as essential ingredients for a life well-lived.

Denver's brunch scene is a vibrant tapestry of diverse flavors from around the world, each dish a testament to the city's multicultural fabric. At Super Mega Bien, Latin American dishes are reimagined through a brunch lens, offering patrons vibrant flavors and traditions spanning continents. The dim sum-style service allows diners to embark on a gastronomic tour, sampling everything from arepas filled with slow-cooked meats to sweet plantain empanadas, each bite a taste of Latin American culture. Similarly, **Onefold**'s menu brings together Asian and Mexican influences, congee, and breakfast tacos side by side, each a testament to Denver's multicultural fabric. This fusion of culinary traditions at the brunch table reflects the city's identity as a melting pot of cultures that finds expression in the most universal language--food.

In addition to those already mentioned, here are some of the fantastic brunch locations worth visiting in Denver:

- **Denver Biscuit Co.:** If you're in the mood for some southern-style comfort food, head to Denver Biscuit Co. This restaurant is famous for its huge, flaky biscuits that are served with a variety of fillings, from fried chicken to bacon and eggs.
- **Jelly Cafe:** This quirky cafe is a local favorite, thanks to its colorful decor and creative menu. Try the "Morning After" burger, which features a beef patty topped with bacon, cheddar cheese, and a fried egg.
- **The Universal:** This cafe serves a variety of classic brunch dishes, from eggs benedict to waffles and bacon. It also has a great selection of coffee and tea drinks to pair with your meal.
- **Root Down:** For a more upscale brunch experience, head to Root Down. This restaurant serves unique brunch dishes, like the vegan benedict (made with tofu and vegan hollandaise) and the smoked salmon hash.

No matter where you go for brunch in Denver, you will find delicious food and a welcoming atmosphere. Just be sure to arrive early, as many restaurants can get quite busy on the weekends!

In Denver, brunch has transformed into a rich mosaic of flavors, seamlessly weaving together the city's historical  essence and contemporary vibrancy. It represents a moment where innovation meets tradition, time-honored classics are infused with fresh perspectives, and novel ideas are welcome. In the city's eateries and cafes, brunch is not just a meal -- it is a narrative of transformation, a celebration of diversity, and a testament to the creative spirit that defines Denver. Picture yourself in a sunlit cafe, the aroma of freshly brewed coffee mingling with the sizzle of bacon, as you savor a plate of pineapple upside-down pancakes, each bite a burst of sweet and tangy flavors. This is the Denver brunch experience, a journey of culinary discovery and delight.

FOOD TRUCKS & STREET FOOD: DENVER'S MOBILE CUISINE

A thrilling adventure awaits in the heart of Denver as a one-of-a-kind food truck scene flourishes, infusing the streets with the scents and tastes of traditional and innovative dishes. Like nomadic chefs, these mobile eateries traverse the city, transforming ordinary corners into vibrant hubs of culinary exploration. The essence of Denver's street food culture lies in its unique ability to satisfy hunger and reflect the city's dynamic spirit. This moving feast caters to the ever-evolving palates of its residents, inviting them to embark on a gastronomic journey like no other.

The annual street food festivals and gatherings punctuating Denver's calendar are not just culinary extravaganzas but also powerful catalysts for community and togetherness. Here, the city's food trucks converge, transforming parks and plazas into vibrant mosaics of flavors and scents. The Denver Street Food Fest is a standout, a yearly celebration that unites the community in a shared space of taste and discovery. Here, visitors wander, plates in hand, moving from one truck to another, each stop a new chapter in their gastronomic adventure. These festivals not only showcase the diversity of Denver's street food scene but also foster a sense of unity. The entire city is invited to feast at this communal table, fostering a sense of belonging and togetherness.

Innovation is the lifeblood of Denver's food trucks, where chefs constantly push the boundaries of flavor and ingredients, blurring the line between gourmet cuisine and street food accessibility. Trucks like **Quiero Arepas**, with its Venezuelan-inspired menu, and **The Ginger Pig**, known for its Asian street food flair, exemplify this creative spirit. They craft dishes that blend authenticity and innovation, offering arepas bursting with savory fillings and bao buns that explode with bold flavors. This culinary creativity enriches Denver's food landscape and challenges diners to rethink their notions of gourmet dining.

Locating these culinary treasures as they traverse the city's streets has become a pursuit for food enthusiasts, a treasure hunt guided by the digital age. Several apps are dedicated to tracking Denver's food trucks, but some popular ones are *Truckster*, *Roaming Hunger*, and *Street Food Finder*. These apps provide real-time locations and menus of the food trucks, making it easy for hungry explorers to find their next great meal. Social media platforms buzz with updates and announcements, and food truck parks like **Denver's Milk Market** become gathering points for those searching for a diverse dining experience. These tools and spaces simplify the search for good food and create a community around Denver's street food scene, connecting diners with the stories behind the dishes they savor.

In the orchestration of Denver's mobile cuisine, where the city becomes a dining room, the food truck scene stands as a testament to the ingenuity and resilience of its culinary community. With their diverse offerings and innovative approaches,  these mobile eateries embody the essence of Denver's gastronomic culture. This landscape thrives on exploration and connection. The streets of Denver, lined with trucks serving everything from gourmet tacos to artisanal ice cream, invite both the curious and the connoisseur to partake in a dining experience that transcends the conventional, a journey through flavors that capture the spirit of the Mile High City.

Here are just a few more of the tasty food trucks you might want to try during your visit:

- **Adobo Food Truck** serves delicious Filipino fare, including lumpia, adobo chicken, and pancit noodles.
- **Baba's Falafel** offers authentic Middle Eastern dishes such as falafel wraps, shawarma, and hummus.
- **The Biscuit Bus** is the go-to spot for Southern-style breakfast sandwiches and biscuits, like the "Biscuit Bomb" with fried chicken, bacon, and cheese.
- **Hey PB&J** offers an elevated twist on the classic peanut butter and jelly sandwich. Try the "Bananas Foster" with caramelized bananas and hazelnut spread.

- **The Rolling Italian** offers classic Italian dishes like meatball subs, chicken parmesan, and Italian sausage sandwiches.
- **Street Frites** offers creative takes on classic French fries, like truffle fries with parmesan and rosemary or loaded fries with chili and cheese.

FARM-TO-TABLE: DENVER'S SUSTAINABLE EATERIES

In the lush state of Colorado, where the soil is abundant with life and the changing seasons dictate the rhythm of life, a movement is flourishing that is rooted in the principles of sustainability and community. The farm-to-table initiative in Denver is not just a whisper of change but a loud roar that demonstrates the city's unwavering commitment to ethical eating and the celebration of local produce. This movement sees chefs and restaurateurs building relationships with farmers, the land, and the seasons. Each dish is a tribute to the environment and the intricate work that it involves.

Restaurants like **Fruition Restaurant** are at the forefront of this culinary revolution, and their menus display Colorado's agricultural wealth. These establishments, led by visionary chefs like Alex Seidel, are pioneers of a dining experience where each ingredient tells its story, from soil to plate, of care, nurture, and respect. Places like Fruition are not just restaurants but a realm where the connection between the eater, farmer, and chef is celebrated, and every meal is an act of shared responsibility towards the land and its gifts.

The menus of these sustainable eateries change with the rhythm of the seasons, adapting and evolving as the earth tilts and turns. In spring, dishes are made with tender greens and crisp radishes that signify the season's arrival. In autumn, plates are filled

with hearty squashes and root vegetables that speak of the earth's last bounty before the winter sleep. Within the framework of seasonal menus, it is here that the true artistry of the farm-to-table movement reveals itself, each dish a testament to the ephemeral beauty of nature's offerings.

An essential aspect of Denver's farm-to-table eateries is their educational component, a commitment to enlightening diners about the origins of their food. At restaurants like **The Kitchen**, diners are not just there for a meal but also immersed in a narrative of cultivation and care. These restaurants bridge the gap between consumer and producer, offering insight into the processes that bring food from farm to table. This education transcends the culinary, instilling a sense of stewardship and a deeper appreciation for the land and its caretakers. Through conversations sparked at the table, diners leave not just satiated but enlightened, armed with the knowledge of their food's journey and the impact of their culinary choices, empowering them to make more informed and sustainable food choices that can make a difference.

Within Denver's dynamic dining landscape, the farm-to-table initiative goes beyond just providing nourishment; it plants the seeds of transformation, nurturing a community deeply connected to the land and its yields. These sustainable eateries, with their chef-driven initiatives, seasonal menus, and educational endeavors, cultivate not just crops but a culture of mindful eating and ethical consumption. They stand as beacons of hope in a world often disconnected from the sources of its sustenance, reminding all who partake of their offerings of the beauty, responsibility, and joy inherent in eating locally and sustainably.

Here are more restaurants in Denver that offer farm-to-table cuisine:

- **Bar Dough** is an Italian restaurant showcasing handmade pasta, wood-fired pizzas, and seasonal dishes from locally sourced ingredients.
- **Basta** celebrates the best of Colorado's agricultural bounty. Their

menu features wood-fired pizza, house-made pasta, and seasonal dishes from locally sourced ingredients.

- **Beast + Bottle** highlights locally sourced meats, vegetables, cheeses, and house-made charcuterie.
- **Black Cat** offers a seasonal menu inspired by the farm's bounty. Their menu features dishes made from locally sourced ingredients, including meats, vegetables, and cheeses.
- **Cafe Aion** features seasonal dishes from locally sourced ingredients, including meats, vegetables, and cheeses.
- **ChoLon** features Asian-inspired dishes from locally sourced ingredients, including meats, vegetables, and seafood.
- **Jax Fish House & Oyster Bar** is a seafood restaurant offering dishes from sustainably sourced ingredients and locally sourced meats, vegetables, and cheeses.
- **Mercantile Dining & Provision** is a market, bakery, and restaurant with dishes made from locally sourced ingredients, including meats, vegetables, and cheeses. (Alex Seidel, Chef/Owner of Mercantile Dining & Provision and Fruition Restaurant, was the James Beard Award Winner of Best Chef: Southwest in 2018)
- **Rioja** is a restaurant that features Mediterranean-inspired dishes made from locally sourced ingredients, including meats, vegetables, and cheeses. (Jennifer Jasinski, Chef/Owner of Rioja, Bistro Vendome, and Stoic & Genuine, was the James Beard Award Winner of Best Chef: Southwest in 2013)
- **Stoic & Genuine** is a seafood restaurant made from sustainably sourced ingredients and locally sourced meats, vegetables, and cheeses.

Finally, two Michelin-starred restaurants in Denver that offer farm-to-table cuisine are:

- **Acorn**, mentioned earlier, is a restaurant led by Michelin-starred chef Steven Redzikowski. Their farm-to-table experience highlights the best of Colorado's agricultural wealth.
- **Frasca Food and Wine** is a restaurant led by Michelin-starred chef Lachlan Mackinnon-Patterson. Its menu features Italian-

inspired dishes made with locally sourced meats, vegetables, and cheeses.

GLOBAL FLAVORS: DENVER'S INTERNATIONAL SCENE

In the heart of Denver, where the shadow of the Rockies meets the endless sky, the city's dining scene unfurls like a world map, promising an exhilarating adventure. Each restaurant is a gateway to a distinct culinary tradition, brought to life far from its origins. In Denver's vibrant streets, diners embark on thrilling culinary journeys to far-off places, guided by the transformative power of cooking. Chefs become storytellers, their creations narrating the tales of diverse cultures and communities. These dishes seamlessly integrate into Denver's rich culinary mosaic, inviting you to embark on a journey of exploration and discovery.

World Cuisine and Ethnic Enclaves

Denver's international dining scene is a testament to the city's diversity, offering unique culinary experiences that blend global cultures. From **Sputnik**, where Eastern European flavors are given a modern twist, to **Pho-natic**, which serves Vietnamese pho with a depth of flavor passed down through generations, each restaurant is a unique gateway to a distinct culinary tradition. These establishments share a common theme: authenticity. They are proud repositories of cultural heritage, preserving the culinary traditions of their homelands while also inviting innovation, creating a harmonious blend between the timeless and the contemporary that entices the Denver diner.

Denver is renowned for its diverse neighborhoods, each with a unique rhythm and character. Within these neighborhoods, you can find an array of specific international cuisines that thrive. For instance, strolling down Federal Boulevard, you will encounter a myriad of Latin American flavors, from the zing of Mexican taquerias to the comforting warmth of Salvadoran pupuserias. This street is a gateway to the diverse culinary traditions of Central and South America, inviting travelers on a flavorful expedition. It's not just about the food; it's about the profound cultural significance of these cuisines.

On the other hand, Aurora has blossomed into a hub for Asian cuisine. Its streets are adorned with Korean BBQ joints, Vietnamese bakeries, and Chinese dim sum restaurants, each offering a portal into the rich culinary traditions of the East. These enclaves aren't just collections of restaurants; they're cultural sanctuaries where food serves as a bridge between Denver's diverse communities and the global heritage they carry.

Here are a few more international restaurants to get your bellies chatting before deciding on your next culinary outing!

- **Biju's Little Curry Shop** - This restaurant offers authentic South Indian cuisine, focusing on curries and dosas.
- **Cho77** - A modern Asian restaurant that offers dishes from Thailand, Vietnam, and China.
- **La Abeja** - A Mexican restaurant that serves traditional dishes like chiles rellenos and pozole.
- **Domo** - A Japanese restaurant that offers traditional dishes like sushi, tempura, and udon.
- **Shondiz** - A Persian restaurant that serves traditional dishes like kebabs and stews.
- **Jerusalem Restaurant** - A Middle Eastern restaurant that offers dishes from Palestine, Israel, and Lebanon.
- **Adrift** - A tiki bar that serves Polynesian-inspired dishes like poke bowls and Hawaiian-style pork ribs.
- **Saigon Bowl** - A Vietnamese restaurant that serves traditional dishes like banh mi sandwiches and pho.
- **Ethiopian Restaurant** - An Ethiopian restaurant that serves traditional dishes like injera bread and doro wat.
- **Tommy's Thai** - A Thai restaurant that offers classic dishes like pad thai and green curry.

- **Sushi Den** - A Japanese restaurant that offers fresh sushi and sashimi dishes.
- **Baba & Pop's Pierogi Kitchen** - An Eastern European restaurant that serves traditional dishes like pierogi and kielbasa.
- **Palenque Mezcaleria** - A Mexican restaurant specializing in mezcal cocktails and authentic street food.
- **Avelina** - A Mediterranean-inspired restaurant that offers farm-to-table dishes focusing on local ingredients.

Culinary Tours

Embarking on culinary tours is a great way to uncover Denver's international dining scene. Companies such as **Local Table Tours** offer curated experiences that guide you through the city's streets, with each stop representing a chapter

in Denver's culinary story. You can sample various global flavors, from Ethiopian cuisine's spicy and intricate dishes in Five Points to the robust and earthy flavors of Middle Eastern fare in South Denver. These guided journeys offer more than just food; they also provide valuable insights into the history and culture that shape each cuisine. Culinary tours can create a profound and unforgettable experience by fostering a connection between diner and dish. They allow you to taste the food and understand its stories and traditions, making your dining experience more enriching and memorable.

Fusion Innovations

At the forefront of Denver's culinary evolution, chefs and restaurateurs are redefining the boundaries of traditional cuisines. They create fusion dishes unique to Denver, blending Chinese culinary traditions with a Rocky Mountain twist. These dishes are hard to categorize, but they offer diners a new and exciting exploration of flavor and texture. For example, you might find a dish that combines the delicate flavors of Sichuan cuisine with the smoky richness of Colorado barbecue. These culinary innovations are inspired by cultural traditions and Colorado's local bounty. They reflect Denver's adventurous spirit and its warm embrace of diversity. Denver's culinary scene finds its most creative expression in global flavors and local ingredients. These dishes tell a new story of convergence and fusion, adding a unique chapter to the international culinary narrative.

Denver's international dining scene is not just a testament to the city's history, migration and settlement, tradition, and innovation. It is a living, breathing entity that fosters connection and understanding. Despite their disparate origins, these dishes unite people, sharing meals about much more than sustenance. They offer opportunities for learning and connection, inviting you to participate in this cultural exchange. As you savor each bite, you become a part of the story, participating in the narrative of Denver's diverse culinary scene. Your presence and participation are not just welcomed; they are valued and cherished as you contribute to the rich tapestry of Denver's international dining scene.

As we end this exploration of Denver's global flavors, we are reminded of the power of food to transcend boundaries and bring people together. The city's vibrant and constantly evolving international dining scene reflects not just Denver's multicultural identity and innovative spirit but also its acceptance of cultural differences. Through the shared language of food, Denver continues to weave a narrative of inclusivity and exploration, inviting people from all walks of life to join in a journey that spans continents and cultures, one meal at a time. Your presence and participation are valued and welcomed.

As we move forward, we are reminded of the importance of blending Denver's rich history with its present vibrancy. The spirit of discovery that defines Denver encourages us to look beyond the familiar and explore what makes this city a mosaic of experiences. Each experience invites us to see the world from a new perspective.

BREWERY AND DISTILLERY DISCOVERIES

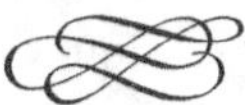

The craft of brewing beer in Denver is more than just production; it's a culture, a community, and a way of life for many. Nestled by the Rockies, this city has become a hub for the craft beer movement where innovation simmers in vats and history is poured into pint glasses. Amidst this renaissance, a network of trails emerges, not of dirt and stone but of hops and barley. These trails connect neighborhoods sewn together by the shared pursuit of the perfect brew. These trails are not just routes but invitations to experience the city's soul, one sip at a time.

CRAFT BEER TRAILS: A DENVER BREWERY TOUR

Trail Itineraries

Picture a delightful Saturday afternoon with the sun casting a warm glow over Denver's skyline. You find yourself in RiNo. The air is infused with the tantalizing scent of malt and hops. It's the perfect launchpad for an exhilarating adventure, navigating streets lined with diverse breweries, each boasting its unique character and beer craft, whether you're seeking out experimental ales at **Ratio Beerworks**, renowned for their music-themed brews, or indulging in barrel-aged specialty beers at **Our Mutual Friend**, the RiNo Brewery Trail beckons, promising a journey through the beating heart of Denver's craft beer scene.

Similarly, the LoHi neighborhood has its path to explore, with establishments like **Little Machine Beer** offering stunning city skyline views alongside award-winning beers. These self-guided adventures are easy to map out with a quick online search. They provide an excellent opportunity to taste Denver's brewing excellence and get a glimpse into the neighborhoods that give the city its vibrant pulse.

Signature Brews

Denver has various beer trails with unique signature brews at each stop. These brews are a testament to the creativity and passion of local brewers who have tried to capture the essence of Colorado's summer fruit harvest or the warm embrace of toasted malt and vanilla, reminiscent of a campfire treat under the starlit Rocky Mountain sky. These signature brews highlight Denver's brewers' skill and connection to the place, with each beer being a love letter to the city and its surroundings.

Brewery Culture

Denver's breweries are more than just places to savor a pint of beer. They are vibrant hubs where culture and camaraderie thrive alongside beer brewing. These breweries host various events, from trivia nights at **Epic Brewing** to running clubs that start at **Joyride Brewing Company** and meander through nearby streets. These gatherings create opportunities for locals and visitors to connect, often accompanied by the inviting aromas wafting from the rolling kitchens of food trucks. The breweries transform into lively social spaces where people share stories over glasses of beer, and friendships are forged in the warm glow of neon signs, fostering a deep sense of belonging and community.

Family-Friendly Breweries

If you plan a family outing to explore Denver's brewery scene, you're in for a treat. Family-friendly breweries like **Great Divide Brewing Co.** are designed to make everyone feel welcome, regardless of age. With spacious taprooms and various non-alcoholic options like craft sodas, these breweries understand that the love for community extends to the youngest among us. It's a common sight to see parents enjoying a leisurely pint while their children are engrossed in coloring or playing board games, adding to the lively ambiance of the place. This inclusive approach reflects Denver's broader ethos, where the art of brewing brings people from all walks of life together, including families.

Some other top Family-Friendly Breweries in Denver Include:

- Denver Beer Co.
- Ratio Beerworks
- Breckenridge Brewery Farm House
- Mockery Brewing

Great American Beer Festival

The Great American Beer Festival (GABF) in Denver is one of the largest beer festivals in the United States. It features some of the best and most diverse craft beer selections. The festival showcases over 4,000 beers from over 800 breweries across the country, including a mix of small and large craft breweries. The festival is an excellent opportunity to explore new and unique craft beers and to learn about the brewing process from industry professionals. In addition to the beer tastings, the festival offers educational seminars, food pairings, and other fun activities.

Some Denver-based breweries featured in the past include **Great Divide Brewing Company**, **Breckenridge Brewery**, **Denver Beer Co.**, **Wynkoop Brewing Company**, and **Strange Craft Beer Company**, among many others.

Several Denver-based breweries have won awards at the Great American Beer Festival (GABF). Here are a few examples:

- **Great Divide Brewing Company** has won dozens of medals, including 18 gold medals. Some of their award-winning beers include Yeti Imperial Stout, Old Ruffian Barley Wine, and Titan IPA.
- **Denver Beer Co.** has won multiple medals, including gold for their Amburana Dream and Graham Cracker Porter beers.
- **Wynkoop Brewing Company** has won several medals, including a gold medal for their Belgorado Belgian-Style India Pale Ale.
- **Strange Craft Beer Company** has won multiple medals, including two silver medals for their Cherry Kriek and Dr. Strangelove Barleywine beers.

These are just a few examples of the many Denver-based breweries recognized for their outstanding beers at the GABF.

DISTILLING DENVER: ARTISAN SPIRITS & WHERE TO SIP

Amid Denver's urban sprawl, a quiet distillery revolution is brewing. This vibrant city has become a hub for craft distilleries that produce everything from whiskies to gins infused with Colorado's wild beauty.

Unique establishments like **Laws Whiskey House** and **Leopold Bros** are at the heart of Denver's distillery scene. These distilleries are about the end product and the grain itself. Heirloom varieties of corn and rye tell the story of place and tradition, each batch distilled into liquid form.

Leopold Bros quietly champions a return to pre-Prohibition era distilling techniques imbued with innovation. Tours offered by these distilleries serve not merely as an introduction to their products but as an education in the distiller's art, from fermentation to aging.

Denver's cocktail bars serve as the stages upon which these local spirits shine. **Death & Co Denver** and **Williams & Graham** offer reverence for the cocktail's craft, and their menus are a testament to the creativity unleashed when artisan spirits meet an artisanal approach.

Denver's artisanal approach to spirit production goes beyond mere distillation; it encompasses sustainability, community, and education. Distilleries integrate practices such as water conservation and waste reduction, and their operations reflect Colorado's deep connection to the land.

Denver's craft distillery scene tells the story of its character—its history, passion for craftsmanship, and commitment to a sustainable future. As these distilleries continue to push the boundaries of the craft, they invite everyone to raise a glass to the spirit of innovation and community that fills the air of Denver.

Here are several of Denver's top craft distilleries you might consider visiting:

- **Leopold Bros.** - This family-owned distillery produces a wide range of spirits, including gin, whiskey, and liqueurs. It is known for its commitment to using organic and locally sourced ingredients in its products.
- **Laws Whiskey House—This award-winning distillery focuses on producing high-quality whiskey using traditional methods. It offers tours and tastings at its** facility in Denver's RiNo neighborhood.
- **Stranahan's Colorado Whiskey**—This iconic distillery is known for its flagship product, Stranahan's Colorado Whiskey, made using locally sourced barley and pure Rocky Mountain water. The distillery in Denver also offers tours and tastings.
- **Bear Creek Distillery**—This small-batch distillery produces a range of spirits, including vodka, gin, and whiskey. It is known for its unique flavor profiles and use of locally sourced ingredients.
- **Mythology Distillery**—This craft distillery is known for its innovative approach to spirit production. It combines traditional and modern techniques to create unique and flavorful spirits, including gin, whiskey, and rum.

- **Rising Sun Distillery**—This family-owned distillery produces a range of spirits, including vodka, gin, and whiskey. It is dedicated to using high-quality ingredients and traditional methods to create its products.
- **State 38 Distilling**—This small-batch distillery is known for its award-winning whiskey, aged in oak barrels and made using locally sourced ingredients. It also produces a range of other spirits, including vodka and gin.
- **Mile High Spirits** - This distillery produces a range of spirits, including vodka, gin, and whiskey. They are known for their unique flavor profiles and use of locally sourced ingredients.
- **Woody Creek Distillers**—This distillery is known for its award-winning vodka, made using locally sourced potatoes. It also produces a range of other spirits, including gin and whiskey.
- **Distillery 291**—This small-batch distillery is known for its award-winning whiskey, which combines traditional and modern techniques. It also produces a range of other spirits, including gin and whiskey liqueurs.

THE RISE OF DENVER'S CIDER HOUSES

A lesser-known but equally vibrant revolution occurs in the dynamic landscape of Denver's craft beverage scene. It's a story woven from the crisp, aromatic essence of apples. This is the rise of craft cider in Denver, a movement that marries the rustic charm of orchard-grown fruits with the innovative spirit of the city's artisans. Across the urban expanse, a handful of cider houses are scattered like seeds, each a testament to a reborn tradition deeply rooted in Colorado soil. These cider houses draw forth a bounty transformed by time, technique, and a touch of alchemy into liquid gold, offering a unique taste of Denver's craft beverage scene.

Craft Cider Boom

Denver's cider renaissance is a journey, transforming from a niche interest to a celebrated craft. It's a tale of cider makers who see the apple as an ingredient and a source of inspiration. **Stem Ciders**, a leading cidery, has become a beacon of the city's cider culture, offering traditional dry ciders alongside experimental batches infused with myriad flavors. Each sip is a testament to the spirit of innovation. This drive to push the boundaries of cider has ignited a similar fervor across the city, from the cozy taproom of **C Squared Ciders** to the expansive patio of the Colorado Cider Company. These spaces blend the ancient art of cider-making with contemporary sensibilities, creating a hub for innovation.

Orchard to Glass

The cider craft in Denver is a testament to locality and sustainability. The journey begins in the orchards of Colorado's Western Slope, where apples are nurtured by dedicated growers. These apples, kissed by high-altitude sunshine, are perfect for cider-making. Each variety is selected for its unique flavor profile. These apples then find their way to Denver's cider houses.

Here, they are crushed, pressed, and coaxed into fermentation. This process, a delicate dance of yeast and sugar, results in ciders as diverse as the apples from which they are derived. Each batch reflects the land and the season. The connection to local growers is a nod to tradition and a commitment to supporting Colorado agriculture. This ensures that each glass of cider tells a story of place, fostering a sense of community and support for local growers.

Cider Tasting Experiences

For those eager to embark on a journey of cider exploration, Denver's cider houses offer tasting experiences that are both an introduction and a deep dive into the craft of cider. For instance, at Stem Ciders' RiNo taproom, cider flights allow for comparisons and discoveries. From the bright tartness of a classic dry cider to the complex layers of a barrel-aged variety, these tastings, often guided by knowledgeable staff, delve into the intricacies of cider. They explore the influence of different apple varieties and the impact of fermentation techniques. These experiences expand the palate and deepen the appreciation for the craft, fostering a community of cider enthusiasts eager to explore the vast range of flavors that cider can offer.

For those wanting to explore cider further, here are the top cider houses in and around Denver:

- **Stem Ciders:** This award-winning cidery has two locations in Denver, one in RiNo and one in Ainsworth. They offer a range of ciders, from classic dry ciders to barrel-aged varieties.
- **Colorado Cider Company:** Located in the heart of Denver, this company is known for its delicious and innovative ciders. It offers a cozy taproom where visitors can sample ciders and enjoy snacks.
- **Wild Cider:** This family-owned cidery in Firestone outside of Denver offers a range of delicious ciders made with locally sourced ingredients. Visitors can enjoy tastings in the cozy taproom or spacious outdoor patio.
- **Haykin Family Cider:** This small-batch cidery in Aurora offers a range of unique and delicious ciders, including hopped and barrel-aged varieties. Its cozy taproom is where visitors can enjoy tastings and learn about cider-making.
- **Big B's Hard Cider:** Located in Hotchkiss, a picturesque town about four hours from Denver, Big B's Hard Cider is worth the drive. They offer a range of delicious ciders made with locally sourced apples, and visitors can enjoy tastings in the beautiful orchard.

Pairing Cider with Food

The art of pairing cider with food is a fascinating aspect of Denver's cider culture. When cider houses like **Acreage** by Stem Ciders design their menu, they carefully consider how to complement their cider offerings with a range of dishes that enhance the overall dining experience. From rich, savory meats to light, fresh salads, the acidity and fruit notes of the cider find their perfect match in each dish, creating a delightful culinary ballet that showcases complementary and contrasting flavors. Denver's cider makers encourage this pairing exploration, inviting diners to view cider as a drink and an integral part of the dining experience. By doing so, cider can enhance and transform the flavors on the plate.

BREWERY TOURS: BEHIND THE SCENES OF DENVER'S BEST

In the heart of Denver, where the majestic Rockies cast their shadow and the air is filled with the promise of adventure, the city's breweries serve as temples devoted to the ancient art of brewing. These spaces, vibrant with the essence of hops and grains, invite visitors to explore the magic of beer making. The tours offered within these sacred walls are more than just strolls; they are gateways to the world of creativity and tradition, where the mysteries of the brew are revealed.

Exclusive Access

Exploring Denver's most celebrated breweries is like being handed the key to a hidden kingdom. With its sprawling campus on the city's outskirts, **Breckenridge Brewery** offers an intimate glimpse into the scale and intricacy of beer production. Guests are ushered through a landscape usually the sole domain of brewers, from towering fermenters to the labyrinth of piping that snakes through the facility.

Similarly, **Great Divide Brewing Co.** opens its production area for visitors, revealing a space where innovation and efficiency converge. The sparkle of stainless steel under the soft glow of overhead lights, the hum of machinery, and the air, thick with the scent of malt, combine to create an atmosphere charged with potential. These tours, often led by people who spend their days coaxing flavors from grains and hops, provide a unique perspective on the art and science of brewing.

Meet the Brewers

One of the most exclusive aspects of going on a behind-the-scenes brewery tour is the rare opportunity to meet the passionate brewers and artisans who devote their lives to crafting beer. For instance, at **Wynkoop Brewing Co.,** a pioneering brewery in Denver, visitors might have the privilege of conversing with a brewer while leaning against a polished bar top, discussing the intricacies of their latest creation. These interactions help to make the brewing process more tangible and real, transforming it from an abstract science into a unique expression of passion and creativity. Shared anecdotes about the long nights of fermentation or unexpected mishaps that led to new flavor nuances create a vivid backdrop that enhances every taste. In these moments, beer becomes more than its ingredients—a narrative of human endeavor.

Educational Value

Denver's brewery tours are a journey of discovery, unfolding like a captivating mystery. Each stop reveals a new layer of the beer-making process, from yeast's role in fermentation to hop varieties' impact on aroma and bitterness. Visitors are not just observers but active participants in a world that seamlessly blends tradition with innovation. **The Tivoli Brewing Co.,** operating out of one of Denver's oldest breweries, offers a historical angle that links present techniques to the legacies of past brewers. Here, amid the relics of brewing history, the continuum of the craft becomes apparent, connecting generations of beer makers. This blend of education and storytelling transforms the tour into an immersive learning experience, engaging the mind as thoroughly as the palate.

Souvenir Tastings

Denver's brewery tours offer a unique experience that usually culminates in exclusive tastings. These sessions often unveil unique brews not available elsewhere, crafted for the curious and connoisseurs alike. At **River North Brewery,** the tasting room offers a wide range of flavors, including barrel-aged wonders and experimental ales such as their popular 'Hazy Hops' IPA and 'Cherry Bomb' sour ale. The tastings are conducted by experts who guide visitors through the brewing and share insights into the flavor profiles and techniques used to create each pour.

Through these tastings, visitors get a complete understanding of the craftsmanship and dedication that drives Denver's brewing community.

Denver's brewery tours are more than just opportunities to taste beer; they are multifaceted experiences that offer access, education, and the pleasure of tasting all in one. They not only provide windows into the craft of brewing but also serve as doorways to a community of beer lovers. These tours reveal the breweries as beer producers and custodians of a tradition that continues to evolve. Visitors are invited to join in the perpetual dance of creation and discovery, making Denver's brewery tours an unforgettable experience.

TAPROOM TASTINGS: A GUIDE TO DENVER'S BEST POURS

Denver's taprooms have an inviting, eclectic ambiance that reflects the city's diverse and pioneering spirit. These communal havens offer warmth beyond the physical comfort of rustic wood and soft lighting. They provide an atmosphere of anticipation as locals and visitors come together, attracted by the allure of craft beer. Conversations flow as freely as the beer on tap, and each table represents Denver's inclusive and exploratory culture. Taprooms serve as a melting pot where the collective pleasure of beer tasting intertwines with the dynamic pulse of city life, weaving a rich mosaic of communal experiences and connections. It's not just about the beer but also the friendships and memories made over a pint.

The allure of rotating taps heightens the taproom experience. Establishments like **Fiction Beer Company** and **Ratio Beerworks** are celebrated for their quality brews and ever-changing selection, ensuring that every visit unveils a new liquid narrative to explore. This constant innovation keeps the taproom experience fresh, encouraging regular pilgrimages to taste the latest creations from the brewers' alchemical labs. The thrill lies in the unpredictability, in the chance to taste a limited-run experimental ale or a seasonal brew that captures the moment's essence. It is a system that rewards the adventurous and keeps the bonds between brewer and community are tightly woven, with each new tap representing a chapter in an ongoing dialogue of taste and craftsmanship.

Denver's taprooms go beyond the simple joy of tasting and elevate the experience through a focus on beer education. Establishments like **Bierstadt Lagerhaus** and **TRVE Brewing** take pride in their role as educators, offering flights accompanied by detailed tasting notes that delve into the nuances of each brew. Staff members, often as passionate about beer as the brewers themselves, are eager to share their knowledge, guiding patrons through the complexities of flavor profiles, brewing techniques, and the storied histories of beer styles. This approach transforms the taproom from a mere venue for drinking into a classroom without walls, where learning enhances enjoyment, and every pint is an opportunity to deepen one's appreciation for the craft.

Pairing events further enrich the taproom experience, marrying the art of brewing with the culinary arts to create symphonies of flavor. Denver's taprooms collaborate with local artisans and chefs to host evenings where beer and food are intertwined in a dance of complementary and contrasting notes. At **Crooked Stave**, for example, beer and cheese pairings unravel the intricate relationships between the fermentation funk and the creamy whispers of artisanal cheese. Meanwhile, events like beer dinners showcase the versatility of beer as a culinary component, with each course a testament to the creativity that flourishes when brewers and chefs unite. These gatherings are not just meals but explorations of the sensory interplay between palate and plate, a celebration of local produce, and the communal act of breaking bread.

The straightforward pleasure of beer tasting transforms into a multifaceted adventure within Denver's lively taproom scene. From the inviting atmosphere that fosters community to the rotating taps that promise perpetual discovery, from the commitment to education that deepens understanding to the pairing events that tantalize the senses, Denver's taprooms offer a microcosm of the city's broader ethos. It is a realm where tradition and innovation intersect, where every pint served is a nod to the past and a toast to the future.

As we close this exploration of Denver's vibrant taproom culture, we are reminded of the simple truth that beer, much like the city itself, is a conduit for connection. The conversations sparked over a flight of beers in the shared moments of discovery. In the communal gatherings that celebrate the craft, we find the essence of Denver's spirit—a community bound by a love for exploration, a passion for craftsmanship, and an unyielding commitment to inclusivity. Here, within the walls of the city's taprooms, the craft beer revolution unfolds, inviting all to partake in the journey, one pour at a time.

URBAN EXPLORATION: NEIGHBORHOOD GEMS

In the heart of Denver, where the present and past merge in the shadows of the Rockies, lies the neighborhood of LoDo, a living testament to the city's ability to reinvent itself while honoring its roots. Once the original settlement of Denver, this area has undergone a renaissance, transforming from a cluster of warehouses and abandoned buildings into a vibrant cultural and nightlife hub. LoDo's streets, lined with red brick buildings that whisper tales of the Gold Rush era, now echo with lively conversations, clinking glasses, and the soft hum of the city at night. Here, history is preserved and lived as a backdrop to the modern vibrancy that defines Denver's oldest yet most dynamic neighborhood. It's a place that demands respect and appreciation for its rich history and its journey to become what it is today.

LODO'S RENAISSANCE: NIGHTLIFE AND HISTORY

Historic Meets Modern

LoDo's transformation is a captivating tale of revival. The district intertwines historic architecture with contemporary culture, creating a neighborhood rich in history and entertainment. As you venture through LoDo, you'll discover Victorian buildings that have withstood the test of time. They now house chic lofts, bustling restaurants, and avant-garde art galleries, sure to ignite your curiosity. The juxtaposition of old and new is evident, with each brick and beam holding a unique story of Denver's past. LoDo beckons you to uncover its secrets and embark on a thrilling journey through its history. Every corner has a history waiting to be discovered by those who dare to explore its streets, inviting a sense of adventure with every step.

Bar Hopping and Brewery Tours

As the sun sets, Lower Downtown (LoDo) in Denver, Colorado, undergoes a stunning metamorphosis. This district's historic allure gives way to a vibrant nightlife scene that offers many local and tourist experiences.

One of the best places to start your evening in LoDo is the **Terminal Bar** in Union Station. The bar's atmosphere is reminiscent of a bygone era, with its high ceilings and classic decor. Here, you can indulge in a vast selection of local Colorado craft beer, sure to delight your taste buds.

If you're looking for a place to take in the stunning views of the city lights against the majestic mountains, then The **ViewHouse is** the perfect spot. This bar offers a rooftop patio, which affords panoramic views of the city skyline. You can enjoy your drinks while taking in the breathtaking scenery.

For those curious about brewing, a visit to **Wynkoop Brewing Company**, Denver's pioneering craft brewery, is a must. You can tour the facility and learn about the brewing process. The brewery also offers a range of delicious beers you can sample and enjoy.

If you're feeling adventurous, check out some of LoDo's speakeasies, such as **Williams & Graham** and **Green Russell**. Williams & Graham has a bookshelf that doubles as a hidden door to the bar, where you can enjoy classic cocktails and an intimate ambiance. Meanwhile, Green Russell is a prohibition-style bar that offers a unique and immersive experience, complete with dim lighting and classic cocktails served in vintage glassware.

Exploring LoDo's many bars and eateries is a delightful experience. Each establishment has its unique charm waiting to be discovered. LoDo has something for everyone, from hidden speakeasies to trendy rooftop bars and craft breweries.

Whether you're a local or a tourist, a night out in LoDo promises to be unforgettable.

Union Station as a Landmark

The station's **Great Hall** is the first thing visitors see upon entering. It is a grand space that serves as Denver's "living room." The hall is home to various shops, cafes, and restaurants catering to all tastes. There's something for everyone here, from local artisanal shops to high-end boutiques.

Union Station is a mecca of culinary delights for food lovers. The station is home to some of Denver's most popular restaurants, including Mercantile Dining & Provision, an award-winning restaurant serving farm-to-table cuisine, and Stoic & Genuine, a seafood restaurant offering fresh, sustainable seafood.

The station also houses several cafes and bars, including the **Pigtrain**

Coffee Company, which specializes in locally roasted coffee and fresh pastries, and **Terminal Bar**, which offers craft cocktails and local beers.

Union Station's transformation from a simple transit point to a vibrant social and cultural center is a testament to LoDo's revival. The station's original architecture has been carefully preserved, while contemporary design elements have been added to create a timeless and modern space.

Overall, Union Station welcomes everyone. Whether you're a traveler looking for a place to relax, a foodie looking for some of Denver's best cuisine, or a local looking for a place to socialize, Union Station has something for you.

Walking Tours

If you're looking to explore the charm of LoDo, there's no better way than to go on a walking tour. These tours are carefully curated to reveal the fascinating stories behind the historic landmarks and brick facades of this unique part of Denver. By peeling back the layers of Denver's history, you'll find yourself transported back in time, imagining the activity of the former transportation hub, the **Market Street Station**, or strolling through **Larimer Square**, where the city's first post office, bank, and theater once stood.

These guided walks are informative and immersive, offering an insight into the narrative of LoDo. You'll connect the past with the present, showcasing Denver's transformation, and learn how this fascinating neighborhood has evolved.

Moreover, each step you take on these guided tours will spark excitement and adventure, making for an unforgettable experience. You'll get to witness the beauty of Denver's rich history firsthand and learn about the people and events that shaped this iconic neighborhood. So, if you're looking to delve into the past and experience the magic of LoDo, then be sure to book a walking tour and explore this enchanting part of Denver.

CHERRY CREEK: SHOPPING AND SERENITY

Under the vast expanse of the Colorado sky, Cherry Creek stands as a testament to elegance and tranquility in Denver. This district is renowned for its high-end boutiques, art galleries, and well-known national brands. It offers a meticulously walkable outdoor setting, inviting visitors to delve beyond mere shopping and immerse themselves in an experience of urban serenity. With its perfect blend of retail luxury and serene landscapes, Cherry Creek provides a sanctuary for those yearning for a peaceful respite from the city's hustle and bustle. It is set against a backdrop that harmonizes urban vibrancy with natural calm, making it an ideal destination for everyone.

Upscale Shopping Experience

Cherry Creek is Denver's most distinguished shopping district, offering a luxurious retail experience that promises to unveil hidden treasures. Each store presents a gateway to a world of elegance and refined taste, from Parisian haute couture to Milanese leather craftsmanship. When strolling through the district, one can discover a handpicked selection of boutiques and galleries that celebrate the art of personal adornment and home decoration with a keen eye for beauty and an appreciation for quality. The outdoor promenade, adorned with aspen trees, provides a shopping experience that is as much about the atmosphere as the pursuit of luxury. It is a testament to Cherry Creek's status as a bastion of upscale consumerism.

Cherry Creek Trail

The Cherry Creek Trail winds through the heart of the district, offering a peaceful respite from the opulence of the shopping experience. It's a quiet ribbon that cuts through the urban fabric, where joggers, cyclists, and anyone seeking peace can find refuge from the city's hustle and bustle. The trail follows the creek's meandering course, offering breathtaking vistas of rippling waters framed by lush greenery. Along the trail, the city's pulse slows, allowing for a communion with nature that refreshes the spirit and invigorates the body. It's a perfect reminder that the call of the wild is always close to Denver's thrum of urban life. It provides a balance that nourishes the need for excitement and the yearning for serenity.

Dining and Cafes

Cherry Creek is a foodie's paradise, with various dining and cafe options catering to every taste and preference. The district is known for its diverse culinary landscape, which blends sophistication with warmth to create a unique dining experience.

Cherry Creek's restaurants will impress if you're in the mood for a gourmet meal. From intimate bistros serving modern interpretations of classic French cuisine to vibrant eateries celebrating the flavors of the Mediterranean with zest and flair, there's something for everyone. Some of the top restaurants in the district include quality establishments like **Elway's**, **Matsuhisa**, and **Departure**.

For those looking for a more relaxed atmosphere, the district's cafes are the perfect place to unwind with a cup of coffee or tea and a delicious pastry. With sun-drenched patios and inviting interiors, these cafes offer a laid-back ambiance perfect for catching up with friends or getting some work done. Some of the most popular cafes in Cherry Creek include **Aviano Coffee** and **Ink! Coffee**, **Crema Coffee House**, **The Molecule Effect**, and **Amethyst Coffee Company**.

No matter where you dine in Cherry Creek, you can expect a culinary journey that celebrates the creativity and skills of Denver's culinary artists. Each meal is a unique experience that complements the district's ethos of luxury and leisure. So whether you're in the mood for a gourmet dinner or a relaxed coffee break, Cherry Creek will satisfy your culinary desires.

Art and Culture

The Cherry Creek district is known for its vibrant art scene that adds depth to its identity. The streets are adorned with public art installations, providing a creative encounter that ranges from whimsical sculptures to thought-provoking murals. The district's galleries house collections that span the spectrum from contemporary works by local artists to masterpieces recognized globally. Moreover, the annual **Cherry Creek Arts Festival** transforms the district into an open-air gallery where artists and art enthusiasts gather to celebrate creativity that blurs the lines between observer and creator. This commitment to fostering an environment where art thrives testifies to Cherry Creek's role as a shopping destination and a cultural hub. The district is a microcosm of Denver's larger narrative as it blends the cosmopolitan with the pastoral and the contemporary with the timeless. Amidst the clatter of heels on cobblestones and the gentle rustle of aspen leaves, Cherry Creek provides a haven for those who seek the essence of Denver's refined yet grounded spirit.

TENNYSON STREET: CULTURE AND CRAFTS

Tennyson Street, nestled in the heart of the Berkeley neighborhood, is a vibrant community with creativity, culture, and heritage. The street, a perfect blend of art and community, offers a delightful experience to all its visitors. It's a place that engages all your senses, from the bohemian artistry that adorns its walls to the aroma of freshly brewed coffee that fills the air. What sets Tennyson Street apart is its unique collection of independent shops, art galleries, and craft studios, each a window into the aspirations and dreams of the local artisans. Tennyson Street doesn't just welcome visitors; it envelops them in an ambiance of imagination and creativity, inviting them to be a part of the narrative and break free from the mundane.

Bohemian Vibe

Tennyson Street's charm lies in its effortless blend of the eclectic and intimate. Walking down this lively avenue reveals a mosaic of experiences, from the whimsical to the profound. Craft studios with their windows adorned with the latest creations give onlookers a glimpse into the meticulous process of making and invite them to appreciate the beauty of craftsmanship. Art galleries serve as sanctuaries of expression, with walls adorned with pieces ranging from the abstract to the realistic, each telling a story without uttering a single word. This atmosphere of artistic freedom and expression fosters a sense of belonging, a reminder that creativity knows no bounds and everyone is a part of the narrative Tennyson Street weaves.

First Friday Art Walks

On the first Friday of every month, Tennyson Street transforms into a living canvas, a vibrant celebration of art, music, and community that illuminates the night. Galleries and studios open their doors wide, inviting the curious and enthusiasts alike to wander and discover. The air is filled with the buzz of live music, its melodies serving as a fitting soundtrack to an evening of exploration. These Art Walks are not just events but a testament to the vibrant cultural fabric that defines Tennyson Street. They are a monthly ritual that unites the neighborhood in a shared appreciation for the arts. On these nights, the street transforms into a river of light and sound, carrying anyone caught in its current. It's a communal voyage through the heart of Denver's artistic soul. This experience will leave you inspired and eager for more.

Craft Breweries and Eateries

This area is home to a number of craft breweries and eateries that offer a unique experience to visitors. The craft breweries in this area are particularly popular among locals and tourists. For instance, De Steeg Brewing is a must-visit brewery known for its blend of quality and quirkiness. The brews served at De Steeg Brewing reflect the neighborhood's inventive spirit and offer a taste of Colorado's artisanal beers.

Apart from craft breweries, the eateries in the area are equally impressive and serve as gathering spots for the community. These restaurants offer delicious plates that are works of art. The Royal is an eatery that exudes rustic charm and offers a unique dish called "Colorado Lamb Shank," which is to die for. The lamb shank is slow-cooked to perfection and served with mashed potatoes and roasted vegetables—a perfect dish to warm you up on a chilly evening!

Another popular eatery on Tennyson Street is **Vital Root**. Known for its vibrant flavors and healthy cuisine, Vital Root offers a unique dish called "Roasted Beet Salad". The salad is a refreshing mix of roasted beets, caramelized onions, goat cheese, and arugula. It is served with a side of citrus vinaigrette that perfectly complements the earthy flavors of the beets.

In summary, Tennyson Street's culinary offerings invite diners on a gastronomic journey that celebrates the bounty of Colorado and the creativity of its chefs. Whether you're a foodie or a beer enthusiast, Tennyson Street has something for everyone.

Historic Charm

Tennyson Street, a gem in the Berkeley neighborhood, is a captivating fusion of history and modernity. Its streets are a picturesque blend of charming bungalows and Victorian houses, starkly contrasting the contemporary artistic and culinary  ventures that have found a home here. This unique juxtaposition of old and new is a living testament to the neighborhood's evolution, a vibrant reminder of its rich past and dynamic present. The preservation of the historic homes alongside the development of Tennyson Street into a cultural hub is a testament to Denver's commitment to honoring its past while moving towards the future.

The community on Tennyson Street is a thriving hub of creativity and entrepreneurship. Each storefront, gallery, brewery, and eatery has a unique story of passion and perseverance to tell. This street reflects Denver's artistic and entrepreneurial spirit, where the past and present merge seamlessly. With its bohemian atmosphere, regular First Friday Art Walks, and dedication to local crafts and flavors, Tennyson

Street is a neighborhood that celebrates expression, community, and the timeless allure of the historic Berkeley district.

All visitors are welcome to join in the dance of culture and crafts, with the future painted in vibrant hues of imagination and heritage. On Tennyson Street, the heart of Denver beats to the rhythm of creativity, offering a truly unique and unforgettable experience. The community here is not just a backdrop but an active participant in the vibrant tapestry of life, inviting visitors to become a part of the story. Your presence here is not just appreciated; it's integral to the neighborhood's vibrant spirit.

SOUTH BROADWAY: ANTIQUES AND ODDITIES

South Broadway is a unique and vibrant area in Denver. It blends the past's charm with the present's energy to create an exciting atmosphere. Locally known as SoBo, this street is home to Antique Row, which showcases a variety of vintage treasures. As you explore this area, you'll discover the rich history of each object on display. The patina of age and the craftsmanship of long-gone artisans offer a glimpse into the past and make for a fascinating experience.

Antique Row

Wandering through South Broadway's famous Antique Row is like stepping into a time capsule. The shop windows display past curiosities, inviting visitors on a nostalgic journey. Navigating this treasure trove requires patience and a love for the hunt. Here, one might find a first edition of a beloved classic or a mid-century modern chair in pristine condition. Shops like **Turn of the Century Antiques** and **The Annex Antiques & Interiors** are gatekeepers to this realm of memory and charm. Their dolls and vintage jewelry, respectively, add to the allure of this place. For those interested in the peculiar, there are shops specializing in oddities with curios that defy the ordinary. From Victorian mourning jewelry to taxidermy, these items whisper tales of the wild. Antique Row's magic lies not just in the objects themselves but also in the stories they carry. Each purchase adds a piece of history to new hands, a tangible connection to the past.

Alternative Nightlife

South Broadway takes on a new persona as the sun sets, shedding its vintage charm for a lively alternative nightlife scene. The area is dotted with dive bars, live music venues, and avant-garde theaters, each pulsing with the diverse rhythms of Denver's night owls. The historic **Hi-Dive**, with its gritty atmosphere and lineup of emerging artists, is a testament to South Broadway's role in nurturing musical talent, where the raw and refined meet in a symphony of sound. Further down, the **Gothic Theatre**, an art deco masterpiece, hosts performances ranging from indie rock to electronic music, its hallowed walls reverberating with the crowd's cheers. In these venues, the night comes alive, weaving a vibrant tapestry of melodies, luminescence, and movement that unites the diverse and unique individuals connected by the shared love of music and laughter.

Artistic Flair

The South Broadway neighborhood has recently experienced an artistic resurgence, adding a new dimension of vibrancy to its already rich mosaic. The area now boasts street art murals that adorn brick facades, turning it into a lively open-air gallery. These vivid  expressions of creativity are born from local and visiting artists' spray cans and brushes, infusing the neighborhood with color and life. Murals like the one on the side of **Mutiny Information Cafe,** a blend of literary homage and whimsical design, invite passersby to pause, reflect, and engage with the urban canvas. Indie art spaces and galleries are nestled between antiques and eateries and champion the work of Denver's burgeoning art scene, offering platforms for expression as diverse as the community itself. In this realm, art is not confined to galleries; it spills onto the streets, creating a visual dialogue that invites participation and contemplation.

Food Trucks and Casual Eats

The South Broadway area in Denver is a melting pot of diverse cuisine and casual dining options. Food trucks and eateries line the avenue, filling the air with the aromas of sizzling street tacos and sweet barbecue smoke. Maria Empanada stands out with its flaky crust and savory fillings that blend tradition and innovation into an art form. On First Fridays, food trucks park on the curb, where chefs work their culinary magic in front of diners. The community comes together under the string lights to share and savor delicious food, making dining an act of discovery and connection.

South Broadway is where the past and present converge in a celebration of all things eclectic, unique, and vibrant. The streets are painted with artistic flair and full of history and nightlife energy. Antique Row beckons visitors with its whispers of history, while the music and murals add a colorful touch of creativity. The district embraces the diversity of its community and the richness of its heritage, where every corner holds a story waiting to be discovered. Each Tennyson Street and South Broadway visit promises a unique experience you won't find anywhere else.

RINO'S STREET ART AND INDUSTRIAL COOL

RiNo is a neighborhood bursting with life and creativity. Once a desolate industrial area, it has undergone a remarkable metamorphosis, emerging as a hub for urban artists and a sanctuary for creatives who revel in its unique embrace of the avant-garde. The streets narrate the tale of this awe-inspiring transformation, with each mural and piece of public art reflecting the community's journey from decay to dynamism. RiNo has genuinely become an outdoor gallery where art is not confined to galleries but is accessible to everyone, sparking curiosity and inviting exploration for all who visit.

The murals in RiNo are not mere decorations, but rather, they are vibrant conversations between the artists and the community. They are visual expressions that stir, delight, and motivate. Each artwork beckons passersby to pause, contemplate, and connect with the stories woven into the district's fabric. The open-air gallery keeps the pulse of RiNo alive, promising a new revelation at every turn and ensuring that the dialogue between art and observer remains perpetual, fostering a sense of active participation in the artistic narrative.

RiNo's craft beer and distillery scene mirrors the neighborhood's artistic spirit, embodying this creative energy with each local brew and spirit. Establishments like **The Source**, an artisan food market housed in a repurposed foundry, epitomize RiNo's innovative spirit. These spaces serve as the social hub of the neighborhood, where people gather to celebrate the art of craft beverage making. The harmonious coexistence of RiNo's visual and culinary arts creates a district that is not just seen but savored, a sensory delight that epitomizes Denver's progressive approach to culture and creativity, sparking a sense of wonder and inspiration in the audience.

RiNo's dining scene is a hotbed of culinary innovation, where chefs draw on the district's artistic energy to push the boundaries of flavor and presentation. Food halls like **Denver Central Market** offer a microcosm of this culinary diversity. Experimental kitchens and pop-up dining experiences further underscore the neighborhood's role as a culinary trendsetter, where dining becomes an exploration of new gastronomic landscapes.

The creative heart of RiNo beats strongest in its studios and galleries, where artists and makers converge to forge a community dedicated to the pursuit of expression and innovation. Spaces like RiNo Art District's headquarters provide a home for artists to create, exhibit, and foster collaborations and invite locals and visitors to engage with the artistic process. This inclusivity makes them feel a part of RiNo's narrative through galleries, workshops, and studios, fostering a sense of belonging and community.

As the sun sets over the murals that tell the story of RiNo's renaissance, it becomes clear that this neighborhood is more than the sum of its parts. It is a testament to the power of creativity to redefine space, transform the industrial into the inspirational, and foster a community where art and innovation are valued and lived. RiNo embodies Denver's commitment to fostering spaces where creativity thrives, communities come together to celebrate the art of the possible, and the urban landscape becomes a canvas for expression and connection.

In conclusion, RiNo, with its street art explosion, pioneering craft breweries and distilleries, innovative dining, and creative spaces stands as a vibrant testament to Denver's cultural richness. It embodies the essence of Denver's commitment to fostering spaces where creativity thrives, communities come together to celebrate the art of the possible, and the urban landscape becomes a canvas for expression and connection. Denver reveals itself as a city of contrasts, where each neighborhood, like RiNo, contributes to the dynamic mosaic that defines the city's energy and vibrancy.

MUSIC LOVER'S PARADISE

In Denver, music is essential to the city's identity, just like the iconic Rocky Mountains that form its skyline. The melodic strumming of a guitar, the saxophone's deep, soulful wail, and the drum set's rhythmic pulsing are deeply ingrained in the city's essence. Music is a universal language that resonates across Denver's bustling neighborhoods, uniting different communities. The city hosts a rich mosaic of musical experiences, from the cozy jazz clubs with an air vibrating with improvisational riffs to the electrifying indie rock venues with palpable energy. Every performance, whether a solitary busker on a bustling street corner or a glorious concert in a historic theater, encapsulates a note of Denver's eclectic and spirited soul, offering a symphony of sounds that beckons to be explored.

DENVER'S LIVE MUSIC VENUES: FROM JAZZ TO INDIE

Diverse Music Scene

Imagine stepping out into the crisp evening air of Denver, with the city lights forming a stunning backdrop to a night of musical exploration. A wide range of options with different genres is available at your fingertips, each offering a unique experience. For those who love jazz, the historic Five Points neighborhood, once known as the 'Harlem of the West,' still swings with places like **Nocturne**. Here, amid the clinking of glasses and the murmur of conversation, patrons are transported to the golden age of jazz, with each performance paying tribute to the masters while showcasing local talent poised to become legendary in its own right. It's a journey of discovery, a chance to uncover the hidden gems of Denver's music scene.

On the other hand, the indie scene thrives in venues like the **Hi-Dive** on South Broadway, which is a beacon for those who prefer rock music's grit and raw energy. The walls of this beloved dive bar, plastered with posters from past gigs, tell the story of Denver's indie music evolution, a narrative punctuated by the thumping bass and wailing electric guitars. In the dim light and close quarters, fans gather here not just to hear music but to feel it, to let the vibrations of sound waves resonate within them, creating a connection that transcends the moment.

Iconic Venues

Denver's vibrant music scene is not just about the past but about the present and the future. It's about the thrill and excitement of live performances, the energy that fills the air, and the anticipation of what's to come. **The Bluebird Theater**, located on Colfax Avenue, has a glowing marquee that has

attracted many artists on the brink of breaking into the mainstream. **The Gothic Theatre** in Englewood perfectly blends Art Deco elegance and excellent acoustics, making every performance feel intimate no matter where you stand. These venues are not just buildings; they are living testaments to Denver's rich musical history, where past and present converge on stage, witnessed by music enthusiasts seeking the thrill of live performances.

Local Bands and Artists

Denver's music scene is not just about the music; it's about the people who make it. Local artists, each with a unique sound and story, are the heart and soul of Denver's live performances. A walk down Larimer Street is a journey through the city's musical landscape, from the bluesy basement of **Meadowlark Kitchen** to the folk tunes of the **Larimer Lounge**. These artists don't just perform; they share a piece of themselves with the audience, creating a bond that transcends the show. Supporting local talent is more than just attending concerts; it's about becoming part of a community that values creativity and the power of music to bring people together.

Music Festivals

The communal spirit of Denver's music scene reaches its zenith at the city's numerous music festivals. **The Westword Music Showcase** transforms the Golden Triangle into a pulsating hub of music, art, and culture, offering a platform for local bands and headliners to captivate an eclectic audience. Meanwhile, the **Underground Music**

Showcase (UMS) sprawls across South Broadway, turning the area into a vibrant celebration of indie music and artistic expression. Here, amid the buzz of anticipation and the camaraderie of shared musical passion, Denver comes alive, showcasing the diversity and vitality of its music scene. More than events, these festivals are rituals that mark the passage of time in the city's cultural calendar, moments of collective joy that underscore Denver's identity as a haven for music lovers.

RED ROCKS: THE WORLD'S BEST CONCERT VENUE

Nestled within the geological marvel of Red Rocks Park, the amphitheater of the same name stands as a monument not just to the power of nature but to the transcendent qualities of music. This venue, carved from towering sandstone monoliths, offers an unrivaled acoustic experience. In this natural amphitheater, sound waves travel with a clarity and resonance that man-made structures can only aspire to. Here, surrounded by a landscape that stretches as far as the eye can see, audiences find themselves enveloped in sound. Each note seamlessly blends into the vast Colorado sky, creating an immersive auditory experience.

Red Rocks' natural engineering marvel acoustics amplify sound with a purity that adds a new dimension to live performances. This unique auditory experience, coupled with the visual spectacle of sunsets that paint the rocks in hues of orange and purple, cements Red Rocks' status as a venue without peers. Performers, too, recognize the singular nature of this space, often remarking on the profound connection they feel with the audience, a bond forged in the shared awe of the moment. This fusion of sound and scenery, nature and music, elevates a concert at Red Rocks beyond mere performance into something approaching the sublime.

Over the years, Red Rocks has welcomed an array of musical giants, with each concert weaving its unique thread into the venue's vibrant historical fabric. From the iconic 1971 concert by John Denver, whose music seems almost crafted for the Colorado landscape, to U2's electrifying 1983 performance captured in the concert film "Under a Blood Red Sky," the amphitheater has been the setting for moments of musical history. These legendary performances, etched in the memories of those who witnessed them, contribute to the lore of Red Rocks, a venue that is as much a pilgrimage site for artists as it is for fans.

For those drawn to experience the magic of Red Rocks, a few practical tips can enhance the experience. Transportation to the venue, nestled in the foothills of the Rockies, requires planning; options range from driving and parking in the adjacent lots to utilizing shuttle services that offer round trips from Denver. Once there, seating choices span the gamut from the up-close intimacy of the lower rows to the sweeping vistas of the upper tiers, each offering a unique perspective on the spectacle. The key to maximizing the Red Rocks experience lies in preparation; arriving early secures desirable parking and seating and allows time to absorb the natural beauty of the surroundings before the music begins.

For those intrigued by the history of this iconic space, the **Colorado Music Hall of Fame**, located within the amphitheater's visitor center, provides a deep dive into the state's musical heritage, with exhibits on the artists who have shaped its sound. These daytime activities, from the physical exertion of a hike to the reflective journey through Colorado's musical history, complement the concert experience, rounding out a visit to Red Rocks with a fuller appreciation of its significance.

At Red Rocks, the lines between nature and art blur, and each concert is a collaboration between the performer and setting, where the landscape's drama amplifies the music's emotional impact. More than any other, this venue demonstrates the potential for music to transcend the ordinary and become a conduit for a shared experience that resonates deep within the soul. In this sacred space, where the earth forms the stage, every performance reminds us of music's enduring power to unite, inspire, and transform.

UNDERGROUND MUSIC SCENE: DENVER'S HIDDEN SOUND

In the lesser-known corners of Denver, a vibrant pulse and rhythm can be felt, distinct from the mainstream melodies heard in the city's more celebrated venues. This underground music scene is a hidden network of basements, warehouses, and DIY spaces that serve as the crucible for the city's most avant-garde and experimental sounds. Uncovering these hidden venues is a thrilling adventure, revealing a side of Denver known only to the most intrepid music explorers, those willing to venture beyond the familiar and discover the raw, unpolished gems of the local music scene.

Discovering Underground Venues

Delving into the heart of Denver's underground music scene is not a journey that can be plotted on a map. It's a quest that demands a willingness to engage, ask questions, and listen carefully. The adventure often begins in the city's independent record stores or  through hushed conversations in the dim corners of coffee shops. Flyers and word-of-mouth serve as breadcrumbs leading to the next unforgettable performance. Social media also plays a significant role in the search for authentic musical experiences, with secret groups and encrypted messages hinting at locations and lineups, creating a modern-day treasure hunt for those seeking that special moment. These venues, often as transient as the sounds they host, offer a space where music and community mesh, where the boundaries between artist and audience blur in the shared energy of live performance.

Genre Diversity

The underground music scene in Denver showcases the city's diverse musical palette, with a wide range of genres that challenge and inspire its audience. From electronic beats merging with punk's raw energy to folk melodies weaving through experimental noise, every performance is an invitation to expand one's musical horizons. Venues such as **Glob**, a nondescript space known for its avant-garde bookings, become

classrooms where audiences learn the language of Denver's musical underbelly. The diversity of music reflects the city's eclectic taste and fosters an environment where experimentation is celebrated. Genres are not boundaries but starting points for exploration, making Denver a hub for music enthusiasts who want to explore the vast spectrum of sound that music encompasses.

Community and Culture

A strong sense of community is the heartbeat of Denver's underground music scene. This bond is forged through shared experiences, often hosted in venues such as the **Hi-Dive**, **Larimer Lounge**, and **Lost Lake**, that operate on minimal budgets and are fueled by volunteers' passion. These venues are more than just places to play music; they are havens for people living at the fringes of the city's mainstream music scene. The atmosphere at these shows is inclusivity, where newcomers are embraced, and the line between performer and fan is blurred. This culture of support extends to the artists themselves, many of whom cut their teeth on the underground circuit, finding their voice amid the encouragement of their peers and the honest feedback of intimate audiences. In these gatherings, which take place under the low ceilings of basements or the starkness of industrial warehouses, Denver's musical future takes shape, nurtured by a community that values authenticity over acclaim. It's a scene that invites you to discover the next big thing, to be part of something new and exciting.

Up-and-Coming Artists

The Denver underground music scene is a nurturing environment for emerging talent, providing a platform for up-and-coming artists to refine their skills before a discerning and supportive audience. Bands such as **The Velveteers**, who blend rock and blues, and **Church Fire**, who deliver electrifying synth-pop performances, are just a few examples of acts that have progressed from the city's hidden stages to broader recognition. These artists encapsulate the spirit of Denver's underground scene, characterized by resilience, innovation, and an unwavering commitment to pushing the boundaries of music. For those interested in discovering Denver's emerging music stars, these venues are the perfect places to experience the birth of new sounds. Each performance is a glimpse into Denver's ever-changing music scene, offering a firsthand experience of the city's unfolding sonic narrative.

In this underbelly of Denver's music scene, the hidden sound that runs through the city's veins finds its voice. This voice resonates with the raw energy of punk, the experimental sounds of avant-garde electronics, and the soulful melodies of folk, all converging in spaces that defy the norm. Here, amid the shadows of the mainstream, music enthusiasts gather, drawn by the allure of the genuine, the untested, and the revolutionary. This is where Denver's musical heart beats most vibrantly, not on the grand stages of well-lit venues but in the city's hidden corners, where every note played is a testament to the enduring power of sound to connect, challenge, and transform.

THE DENVER MUSIC FESTIVAL GUIDE

Denver's annual music festivals are a vibrant part of the city's cultural calendar, drawing in music enthusiasts and casual listeners alike. Each festival offers a unique blend of genres, from indie rock to jazz, electronic to classical music. These festivals are held in various locations across the city, providing a unique opportunity to experience Denver's eclectic music scene against the backdrop of the city's urban landscape and natural beauty. It's a musical journey that promises to surprise and delight, with each festival offering its distinct blend of sounds and experiences.

Some popular festivals held in Denver include the **Denver Day of Rock**. This one-day event brings the downtown area to life with live rock and pop performances. It is free and serves a philanthropic purpose by supporting local nonprofits. **City Park Jazz**, on the other hand, offers a more peaceful setting. Attendees can enjoy the serene atmosphere of the lush greenery and placid lake while listening to the smooth vibes of local and national jazz acts.

Some festivals are held outside the city, in locations where music and nature blend seamlessly. For instance, the **Telluride Bluegrass Festival** is held in the San Juan Mountains. It features top-tier bluegrass performances against a backdrop of awe-inspiring natural beauty. **The Rocky Mountain Folks Festival** in Lyons is another festival that showcases folk, Americana, and indie music genres, all shared under the expansive Colorado sky.

Attending Denver's music festivals is a rewarding experience that requires some planning. It's a chance to discover new music, enjoy the city's unique atmosphere, and be part of a vibrant community. To make the most of these events, it's advisable to secure tickets in advance, dress appropriately for the weather, and stay hydrated. Being flexible in your schedule allows you to explore new sounds and embrace the moment's spontaneity. Most festivals provide apps or schedules to help you plan your day and ensure you don't miss your favorite performances.

Denver's music festivals also emphasize the importance of local talent and showcase the city's flourishing music scene. Events like the **Westword Music Showcase** offer local bands and DJs the opportunity to perform alongside national headliners, fostering a sense of community and positioning Denver as a nurturing ground for musical innovation. It's a celebration of our city's unique sound, a testament to the talent and creativity that thrives in our community.

The festival season is an integral part of Denver's cultural fabric. It reflects the city's transformation and draws together music lovers from all walks of life. Each festival is unique, weaving into Denver's urban landscape and creating a rhythm that resonates with the city's heart and soul.

CLASSICAL DENVER: SYMPHONY AND OPERA NIGHTS

Classical music thrives in the heart of Denver, where the rhythm of contemporary life harmonizes with a rich cultural heritage. **The Colorado Symphony** and **Opera Colorado**, known for their distinctive fusion of classical and modern performances, stand out as this dynamic scene's pioneers. Nestled within the **Denver Performing Arts Complex**, these institutions serve as a living testament to the enduring allure of orchestral and operatic art forms.

The Colorado Symphony offers a diverse repertoire, from the stirring symphonies of Beethoven to the evocative cinematic scores of John Williams. Led by skilled conductors, the orchestra brings these compositions to life, which have resonated through the ages, telling stories of triumph, tragedy, and transcendence. Similarly, Opera Colorado stages productions that delve into the depths of the human experience, presenting works that stir both the heart and the mind. From the heart-wrenching romance of 'La Traviata' to the uproarious antics of 'The Barber of Seville,' the company's performances pay homage to the operatic tradition while reflecting contemporary themes.

The Denver Performing Arts Complex not only showcases the talents of local and visiting artists but also stands as a symbol of Denver's commitment to nurturing the arts and ensuring that classical music remains an accessible and cherished part of the city's cultural identity. Its halls and theaters provide a space where music transcends its physical boundaries, enveloping audiences in a world where beauty and harmony reign supreme. With its central location and ample parking, the complex is easily accessible to all, making it a perfect venue for a night of classical music.

In addition to the grandeur of performances, the Colorado Symphony and Opera Colorado extend their reach through educational and outreach programs that ignite a passion for classical music among Denverites of all ages. Initiatives like "Tiny Tots" concerts and "Opera on the Go" bring the magic of music to the community, demystifying the classical genre and fostering an appreciation that spans generations. These inclusive programs, often conducted in collaboration with schools and community centers, underscore the belief that classical music is not an esoteric art form reserved for the few but a universal language that speaks to the many, making everyone feel welcomed and encouraged to participate.

Denver's classical music scene offers unique experiences that highlight its versatility and vivacity. Open-air concerts at Red Rocks Amphitheater blend the beauty of nature with the power of music, creating a truly unforgettable experience. Holiday-themed shows, such as 'A Colorado Christmas' and 'Halloween Spooktacular,' infuse the traditional concert format with a sense of whimsy and wonder, promising festive joy. Collaborative performances that bridge genres, featuring artists from jazz, rock, and beyond, exemplify the innovative spirit that propels Denver's classical music scene into new and exciting territories, offering a fresh and thrilling perspective on classical music and leaving the audience intrigued and excited about what's to come.

Denver's love for classical music reflects its broader narrative of a city in love with the arts. It is here, amid the rush of modern life, that the timeless strains of symphony and opera find a home, enriching the cultural landscape and inviting all to partake in the shared music experience. As we turn the page, the journey through Denver's artistic offerings continues, each chapter a discovery of the myriad ways in which this city celebrates the creative spirit.

I n Denver, amidst the cool autumn air and the splendid Rocky Mountains, stands the **Empower Field at Mile High**. This stadium, home to the **Denver Broncos**, is more than just a place to play football; it is a coliseum where modern-day gladiators compete. Empower Field is a testament to Denver's passion for football, with a rich history of legendary games like 'The Drive' in 1987 and unforgettable plays such as 'Fumble' in 1997. These moments, along with heroic comebacks like the 'Miracle at Mile High' in 2012, have not just etched themselves into the hearts of Broncos fans but have become a part of their identity. Every Sunday, as well as the occasional Monday and Thursday night, it transforms into a communal ritual filled with anticipation and unity.

Fans, wearing orange and blue, gather and cheer, creating a palpable energy that embodies the essence of sportsmanship and camaraderie in the Mile High City. It is a place where you are not just a spectator but a member of a vibrant community united by a shared love for the game, a community you are proud to be a part of.

MILE HIGH STADIUM: DENVER'S FOOTBALL FORTRESS

Iconic Venue

Mile High Stadium is not just a significant landmark for the Denver Broncos; it is the heart of a community. It has a rich history and is an essential venue for the team. The stadium's place in the city's identity is undeniable. It is known for being loud and for the sea of orange that floods its stands. This stadium holds a special place among American sports venues. It is a place where football greats have left their mark. Its importance goes beyond the physical structure. The stadium's unique architecture, with its steep seating and open ends, is designed to amplify the crowd's roar, ensuring that every cheer, gasp, and chant resonates within its walls and across the city. This creates a unifying call to arms on game day. The team's resilience and skill inspire the fans, creating a culture of unwavering support and belief in the team's ability to overcome any challenge. This sense of community, of being part of something bigger, makes Mile High Stadium more than just a venue but a home for Broncos fans. The stadium also offers a range of amenities, including comfortable seating, various food and beverage options, and state-of-the-art facilities designed to enhance the fan experience and make every visit memorable.

Game Day Experience

Picture this: the sun setting behind the majestic Rocky Mountains, casting long shadows across the parking lots. The smell of grilled burgers and laughter fills the air, signaling the start of a cherished tradition - tailgating. Here, fans from all walks of life gather hours before kickoff, a community united by their shared devotion to the Broncos. Inside the stadium, the atmosphere crackles with anticipation as the crowd finds its voice, a crescendo of support that reaches its peak at the sight of the home team bursting onto the field. It's a ritual that goes beyond the game itself, encapsulating the joy, the heartache, and the eternal hope of sportsmanship. After the game, win or lose, the

celebration continues. Fans spill out onto the streets, their cheers echoing through the city as they revel in the shared experience and the sense of community that only a Broncos game can bring.

Stadium Tours

If you're a fan of the Broncos and the Mile High Stadium, you can take a behind-the-scenes tour to see and experience the heart of Denver's football culture. Walking through the players' tunnel, you can almost feel the echoes of past glory and the whispers of legends who have worn the orange and blue. The locker room, a sacred place for any fan, reveals the preparation and camaraderie behind every game. You'll also get a chance to step onto the field, providing a rare perspective of the vast expanse where battles of strategy and strength take place. These tours offer more than just a glimpse into this iconic stadium's operation, history, and soul; they provide a way for fans to deepen their connection to the team and the stadium, to feel more involved and engaged in the game day spectacle, and to gain valuable insights that can enhance their fan experience. The tour guides, often former players or team staff, share their personal experiences and anecdotes, giving fans a unique and intimate understanding of the team's history and culture.

Fan Culture

Denver's football culture is not just about the game but about the deep emotional connection between the fans and the team. It's a culture deeply ingrained in its fan base, resulting in a lively mix of tradition, loyalty, and community. On game days, people follow various rituals in bars and living rooms throughout the city. Some wear a lucky jersey, and others gather with friends and family to cheer, celebrate, or commiserate. The 'Mile High Salute, a tradition started by former Broncos

player Terrell Davis, is a common sight in the stands after a touchdown. This simple gesture, a salute to the fans, embodies the spirit of the team and its relationship with its supporters. Throughout football season, fan clubs and community events strengthen the team's and its supporters' bonds, creating a sense of family beyond the stadium. Denver's football culture is such that people talk reverently about games played in the past, pass down the legacy of players like John Elway, Payton Manning, and Terrell Davis through generations, and continue to hope for future triumphs. This unique blend of tradition, loyalty, and community sets Denver's football culture apart, making it a source of pride for Broncos fans.

COORS FIELD: A HOME RUN FOR BASEBALL FANS

Nestled in the heart of Denver, where the urban landscape meets the majestic Rockies, Coors Field stands out as a beacon for baseball enthusiasts. It's not just a stadium but an architectural marvel that offers fans an experience beyond just watching a game. Its design, with open concourses and a classic brick facade, evokes the nostalgia of early baseball parks while embracing the modern fan's desire for comfort and visibility. From every viewpoint within its confines, spectators can enjoy breathtaking views of the diamond where the Colorado Rockies play and the sun setting against the Rockies, painting the sky with colors as vibrant as the game unfolding below. It's a place where every game is a unique experience, where the stunning surroundings and the comfort of modern amenities amplify the thrill of the sport. Coors Field is where baseball fans can immerse themselves in the game, the atmosphere, and the history, creating memories that will last a lifetime.

Coors Field offers attractions beyond the outfield for families venturing into baseball fandom. The interactive area designed for children, known as the 'Kids Zone, 'allows the youngest fans to engage with the sport on their terms. Here, they can try their hand at pitching simulations that spark dreams of big-league glory or step into the batting cages that offer a taste of hitting a home run. The Rooftop, an expansive deck above right field, has revolutionized the concept of socializing at a baseball game, providing a space where fans can enjoy the game and each other's company, all with a backdrop of Denver's skyline and the Rockies. These features underscore the stadium's role as a venue for watching baseball and a community space where memories are made and families come together to celebrate their love for the Rockies and the game. Coors Field is not just a place to watch baseball but a place to be a part of a community and share the excitement and joy of the game with fellow fans and families.

Amidst the cheers and the crack of bats, Coors Field also caters to the palate of the discerning fan. It offers a culinary experience that mirrors the diversity and richness of Colorado's food scene. Gone are the days of baseball fare being limited to hot dogs and peanuts; Coors Field invites fans to indulge in various local eats and craft beers, turning every game into an opportunity for culinary exploration. From gourmet burgers that blend local flavors with classic Americana to tacos filled with locally sourced ingredients, the stadium's concession stands and restaurants provide tastes that elevate the game-day experience. The craft beer selection, featuring brews from across Colorado, allows fans to toast their team's successes with flavors as bold and complex as the game on the field. This commitment to showcasing local cuisine and brews enhances the spectator experience and is a testament to the stadium's integration with the city's vibrant food culture.

Coors Field is more than just a ballpark; it's a microcosm of Denver itself, a place where the spirit of the West meets the passion for baseball, where family and community find common ground in the love of the game. Every pitch thrown and home run celebrated is a testament to baseball's enduring allure. This sport continues to captivate and unite fans across generations.

THE DENVER NUGGETS: BASKETBALL AT ALTITUDE

The Denver Nuggets have established themselves as a basketball powerhouse in the heart of Denver. Ball Arena, where the games are played, is known for its fast-paced and energetic atmosphere inspired by the city's high altitude and the team's dynamic gameplay. The Nuggets are renowned for their resilience and flair and have become an integral part of the city's identity, bringing pride and unity to its residents. The arena buzzes with excitement as fans cheer on their team, creating an atmosphere that is truly electric and unique to the Nuggets.

Playing basketball at altitude presents unique challenges and advantages, a dynamic that Ball Arena embodies with every dribble and every shot that travels noticeably farther than at sea level. This phenomenon, resulting from thinner air, allowing less resistance, turns the game into a high-scoring affair, where three-pointers are more frequent, and the game takes on an elevated sense of excitement. On the other hand, players find themselves adjusting their shooting and endurance in an environment where the ball behaves unpredictably. This interplay between the physics of altitude and the game's skill adds a layer of strategy to each matchup, making Ball Arena one of the most intriguing and high-scoring arenas in the NBA. Ball Arena is a place where basketball fans can witness the game at its most intense and thrilling, where every shot has the potential to change the course of the game, and where the energy in the arena is palpable.

The team's energy is infectious, and fans eagerly anticipate each game. Recent seasons have marked a resurgence of success and talent, with the Nuggets making deep playoff runs and capturing the attention of basketball enthusiasts. Players like Nikola Jokic, known for his versatility and prowess, embody the spirit of the Nuggets through their exceptional performance yet humble demeanor. Their dedication and skill have elevated the team to new heights, making each game a thrilling spectacle for fans.

The team's engagement with fans extends beyond the court, with a range of initiatives and themed events that celebrate the diversity and vibrancy of their supporter base. From Noche Latina, a night that honors Denver's rich Latino community with special jerseys and cultural performances, to Pride Night, an event that raises awareness and support for LGBTQ+ rights, the Nuggets demonstrate their commitment to inclusivity and representation. Community outreach programs that involve players and staff in charity work and youth engagement reinforce the team's bond with the city and its fans, built on mutual respect and shared values.

Ball Arena offers an exceptional fan experience, with amenities designed to cater to every age and interest. From interactive fan zones to upscale lounges that provide a reprieve from the crowd's buzz, the arena ensures that each visit is memorable. Culinary offerings throughout the arena reflect Denver's eclectic food scene, with local vendors serving various dishes far beyond the standard fare.

The Denver Nuggets have a rich history that mirrors the city's evolution. Established in 1967, the team joined the NBA in 1976 and has since seen notable players like Alex English and Dikembe Mutombo leave an indelible mark on its legacy. Milestones like the unforgettable 1994 playoff victory against the top-seeded Seattle SuperSonics, a game that went down in history as one of the greatest upsets, are touchstones of the Nuggets' resilience, inspiring new generations of players and fans alike.

The Nuggets are more than just a basketball team; they symbolize athletic excellence and community spirit in Denver. Each game at Ball Arena celebrates the city's heart and soul, bringing together individuals united by their love for basketball and their team. The team's community engagement, from charity work to youth programs, reinforces their bond with the city and its fans, creating a sense of pride and unity that extends far beyond the court.

THE COLORADO AVALANCHE: HOCKEY IN THE ROCKIES

The Colorado Avalanche has carved a path of exceptional skill and unwavering determination in ice hockey. Their triumphs, marked by multiple Stanley Cup victories, have elevated them to an NHL powerhouse. These victories are not mere records but heart-pounding milestones in their relentless pursuit of greatness. The team's unity and strategy have forged them into a formidable force, ready to take on any challenge. Their matches are not just competitions but adrenaline-fueled battles of will, endurance, and skill, especially when facing off against their rivals, the Detroit Red Wings.

The Avalanche's fans are not just spectators but an integral part of the team's culture, united in their passion for the sport. They come together in pre-game festivities outside Ball Arena, wearing jerseys with their favorite player's name and chanting, "Let's go, Avs!" The team's commitment to the Denver community is also noteworthy, with programs that engage with young enthusiasts and charitable efforts that aim to improve the lives of those in need. This sense of community, of being a part of something bigger, makes being an Avalanche fan so special.

The Colorado Avalanche's story is a testament to the enduring allure of ice hockey. This sport embodies resilience, teamwork, and the unyielding pursuit of victory.

SPORTS BARS: WHERE FANS UNITE

In Denver, sports is more than just a pastime; it's a way of life. The city has several sports bars that serve as a sanctuary for sports enthusiasts to celebrate their team's victories or commiserate during defeats. These bars offer more than just a place to watch the game; they are cultural hubs where people can declare their loyalties, form friendships, and share the game-day experience. They provide an elevated experience beyond watching the game from the comfort of home or the stadium.

Best Sports Bars

Society Sports and Spirits is an excellent place for an immersive viewing experience. The venue has many screens so you will see all the action, and the atmosphere is full of anticipation. It's the perfect place to watch a game with others and feel the highs and lows of every play together. On the other hand, The Cherry Cricket is also a great option, especially for beer lovers. The venue has a great selection of local brews, and the conversations flow as freely as the drinks. The walls are decorated with stories of games past, and the screens light up faces with every touchdown or home run.

Local Favorites

Denver's sports culture is deeply ingrained and celebrated in venues like Stoney's Bar and Grill, which have become integral parts of the city's fabric. The walls of these establishments are adorned with memorabilia that echoes the city's rich sports history. Regulars at these places are not just patrons; they are part of a family, well-versed in the local teams, and welcoming newcomers with open arms. They share in the game day ritual, fostering a sense of belonging that transcends mere fandom. Within these walls, the pulse of Denver's sports passion is palpable, and every game is an event where every patron feels at home.

Game Day Specials

Sports bars are popular places on game day, with their game day specials adding to their allure. Places like Wash Park Sports Alley offer deals that make the experience not just about the game but also about the delicious food accompanying it, such as the aroma of buffalo wings. These specials are often themed around the teams playing, making the experience even more exciting and adding an extra layer of excitement to the proceedings. Watching the game at a sports bar is not just about the score but also about the community and cuisine.

Sports Trivia and Events

For those whose love of sports goes beyond the game, trivia nights and special events offer an opportunity to exercise their minds. Places like The Sports Column host evenings where knowledge of obscure sports facts is the key to victory, creating an environment where competition and learning are intertwined. These events, often marked by laughter and friendly banter, showcase the significance of sports bars beyond just being places to watch games. They serve as places for socializing, competing, and celebrating the diverse and rich sports culture.

In Denver, where sports are a cornerstone of the community, sports bars stand as beacons of camaraderie and competition. They are not just venues but also landmarks in the fandom landscape, where the game lives on screens and in the stories, celebrations, and connections they foster. Here, amidst the clinking of glasses and the shared anticipation of fans, Denver's love for sports thrives, a living tribute to the city's unwavering passion for the game. These sports bars are more than just establishments; they are microcosms of the city's vibrant sports culture, a culture that thrives on the shared experiences of its people.

As the cheers and the clatter of dishes fade into the background, the true essence of these sports bars comes into focus. They are more than just establishments; they are microcosms of the city's vibrant sports culture, a culture that thrives on the shared experiences of its people. In Denver, where the mountains stand as silent witnesses to the city's thriving spirit, these sports bars remind us that regardless of the game's outcome, the unity, the shared moments of joy, and the bonds forged in the crucible of fandom that truly endure.

As we turn our attention away from the screens and venture into the night, the echoes of the day's matches persist, serving as a testament to the community fabric formed by collective enthusiasms and endeavors. In Denver, the love for sports transcends the arenas and fields, finding a home in the hearts of those who gather to watch, celebrate, and remember together.

CONCLUSION

Greetings, fellow explorers and Denver enthusiasts!

Can you believe it? We've explored the one-of-a-kind Mile-High City, a place that offers a myriad of experiences found nowhere else. From its lively streets to serene peaks, Denver has enchanted us with its vibrant art scene, exhilarating outdoor activities, intriguing history, diverse culinary offerings, and exceptional brewing culture. We've shared joy at family-friendly spots, strolled through unique neighborhoods, enjoyed a variety of music, cheered for sports teams, and admired architectural marvels. Who could have imagined a single city could offer such a rich tapestry of experiences?

I poured my heart into showing you the Denver that I have adored. It is not just about the places; it is about the stories they hold, the people who bring them to life, and the hidden gems that wait around every corner. This book was never meant to be a one-size-fits-all guide but rather a treasure map, leading you to create unforgettable moments in Denver.

Now, it's time for you to venture beyond this book's confines and unravel your Denver tale. Let your curiosity guide you as you stumble upon your favorite haunts and hidden treasures, like the charming coffee shop on 5th Avenue or the breathtaking vista from the rooftop bar downtown. And as you do, remember to tread lightly, love deeply, and laugh often.

Our beautiful planet and the communities we visit deserve our utmost respect and care. So, pack your reusable water bottle, support local businesses, and leave no trace as you leave your mark on Denver.

I would be overjoyed to hear about your adventures! Share your stories, photos, and must-see spots on social media using #MyMileHighJourney. Let's keep the conversation going and build a community of Denver enthusiasts passionate about exploration and discovery. Your posts could ignite someone else's journey or spark a new discussion about Denver's hidden gems.

Your insights and experiences are the heartbeat of my work. Your perspective on the Rocky Mountains or another dynamic city could shape the next edition of this guide or inspire a new book. Your contributions are priceless, and I eagerly look forward to hearing about your journeys.

Speaking of what's next, keep your eyes peeled. There is always a new adventure on the horizon, and I'm buzzing with ideas for our next journey together.

As you turn this final page of "Denver Dossier: Themed Adventures for Every Traveler," I hope you're already dreaming of your next journey, inspired by the vibrant narratives and hidden gems we've shared. Your adventure doesn't have to end here, though. By sharing your thoughts, you can guide fellow travelers on their path and keep the spirit of exploration alive.

I invite you to scan the QR Code below and visit Amazon to leave a review of your experience with 'Denver Dossier.' Your feedback is not just valuable; it's crucial. It helps me understand what resonated with you, what captivated you, and how I can make future editions more engaging and helpful for travelers like you. Whether it's a memorable adventure the book inspired you to embark on, a hidden locale you'd never have discovered without it, or any part of the book that struck a chord with you, I'd be thrilled to hear about it.

https://qr.link/GphlvM

By sharing your review, you are not just providing feedback but also contributing to the vibrant community of curious explorers. Your voice is significant, and it plays a role in shaping the future of travel storytelling. Let's continue this adventure together. Scan the QR Code now and share your journey with us through 'Denver Dossier: Themed Adventures for Every Traveler'.

Until then, keep wandering, wondering, and always keep your heart open to the stories that await.

Happy travels,

Kimberly

REFERENCES

RiNo Art District Strategic Plan 2022-2027 https://ctycms.com/co-rino/docs/rino-strategic-plan-2022-2027.pdf

Denver Public Art: Home https://denverpublicart.org/

The Buildings https://www.denverartmuseum.org/en/buildings

Inside Denver's First Friday Art Nights https://www.colorado.com/articles/inside-denvers-first-friday-art-nights

Margaret "Molly" Brown - Colorado Women's Hall of Fame https://www.cogreat-women.org/project/margaret-molly-tobin-brown/#:~:text=Brown%20contributed%20-generously%20to%20needy,was%20Denver's%20first%20preservation%20project.

Denver's "Harlem of the West" https://www.rmpbs.org/blogs/rocky-mountain-pbs/denvers-harlem-of-the-west/

Capitol Hill Neighborhood History https://history.denverlibrary.org/neighborhood-history-guide/capitol-hill-neighborhood-history

In Denver, Balancing Growth and Preservation https://www.marketurbanist.com/blog/in-denver-balancing-growth-and-preservation

Geology of Red Rocks, Colorado - ThoughtCo https://www.thoughtco.com/geology-of-red-rocks-colorado-4122859

Confluence Park https://www.aia.org/design-excellence/award-winners/confluence-park

Best Family Hikes Near Denver, Colorado https://dayhikesneardenver.com/best-hikes-with-kids-near-denver-colorado/

Bike Denver Initiative - Bicycle Colorado https://www.bicyclecolorado.org/initiatives/bike-denver/

Conservation at Denver Zoo https://denverzoo.org/conservation/

Exhibits | Children's Museum of Denver https://www.mychildsmuseum.org/exhibits

Elitch Gardens' Dive-in Movies, Fireworks and Concerts ... https://www.milehighmamas.com/blog/2023/05/31/elitch-gardens-2023-events/

Public Tours https://dinoridge.org/visit-dinosaur-ridge/public-tours/

Denver's 26 Most Iconic Dishes https://denver.eater.com/maps/best-denver-foods-restaurant-dishes

Brunch is back in a big way in Denver, but how did we get ... https://www.denverpost.com/2022/08/17/brunch-denver-new-best-bloody-mary-pancake-flights/

15 of the Best Food Trucks in Denver and Beyond https://www.5280.com/best-food-trucks-in-denver/

14 Farm-to-Table Denver Restaurants Serving the Best Late-Summer Produce https://www.5280.com/14-farm-to-table-denver-restaurants-serving-the-best-late-summer-produce/

Denver's Essential Breweries Right Now, Spring 2023 https://denver.eater.com/maps/best-new-denver-breweries

15 of the Best Denver Distilleries https://www.5280.com/best-denver-distilleries/

The Nine Best Cider Houses in Metro Denver https://www.westword.com/restaurants/the-nine-best-cider-houses-in-metro-denver-10632651

Denver Brewery Tours https://www.denver.org/things-to-do/tours/brewery-tours/

REFERENCES

LoDo, Denver - Wikipedia https://en.wikipedia.org/wiki/LoDo,_Denver#:~:text=LoDo%20(Lower%20Downtown)%20is%20an,in%20urban%20reinvestment%20and%20revitalization.

Cherry Creek Regional Trail - Colorado https://www.traillink.com/trail/cherry-creek-regional-trail/

Inside Denver's First Friday Art Nights https://www.colorado.com/articles/inside-denvers-first-friday-art-nights

4 New Hot Spots Invigorating Denver's Antique Row https://www.5280.com/new-hot-spots-invigorating-denvers-antique-row/

Denver's Musical Past https://tidal.com/magazine/article/denvers-musical-past/1-9074

10 of the most notable performances at Red Rocks - Denver https://kdvr.com/news/local/notable-historical-red-rocks-performances-denver/

The Meow Wolf Guide to the Denver Underground https://meowwolf.com/blob/meow-wolf-denver-underground-guide

Your guide to summer music festivals around Colorado https://www.cpr.org/2023/05/03/colorado-summer-music-festivals-guide/

The "Mile High Salute" is a celebratory tradition started ... https://www.denverbroncos.com/team/tradition/

Rockies Kids | Colorado Rockies https://www.mlb.com/rockies/fans/kids

Community https://www.nba.com/nuggets/community/

Colorado Avalanche | History, Stanley Cup, & Notable Players https://www.britannica.com/topic/Colorado-Avalanche#:~:text=Recent%20News&text=Colorado%20Avalanche%2C%20American%20professional%20ice,%2C%202001%2C%20and%202022).

Colorado State Capitol https://en.wikipedia.org/wiki/Colorado_State_Capitol

Denver Architecture and Design https://www.denver.org/articles/post/denver-architecture-and-design/

CHARACTER-DEFINING FEATURES OF DENVER'S ... https://www.denvergov.org/content/dam/denvergov/Portals/646/documents/landmark/design_guidelines/Character_defining_features/Character_defining_features-Cover.pdf

Before and After: 10 Amazing Examples of Adaptive Reuse in ... https://www.confluence-denver.com/features/adaptive_reuse_101415.aspx

ABOUT THE AUTHOR

Kimberly Cordova has exemplified resilience and adaptability throughout her life. Her journey, a testament to her strength, has taken her through diverse and vibrant landscapes. Originally from La Crosse, Wisconsin, she was raised amidst the awe-inspiring scenery of Denver, Colorado, and now resides in Santa Fe, New Mexico, with her husband, Greg.

At the core of Kimberly's life is her family. For years, she devoted herself to raising her daughter, Channa, as a single mother. It wasn't until her late forties that she embraced matrimony with Greg, starting a new chapter. Together, they cherish their everyday moments and enjoy living in Santa Fe.

Kimberly's daughter, Channa, is married and has blessed Kimberly with two precious grandchildren, Vera and Tillman, whom she lovingly refers to as her "grandsugars" and treasures above all else.

Although Kimberly has decades of experience in the IT/Technology field, her true passions extend far beyond the digital world. She is an avid traveler who has explored many countries, drawing inspiration from their diverse cultures and histories.

Kimberly's life experiences have shaped her diverse interests, each one a window into her vibrant personality. She finds solace and joy in crochet, indulges her curiosity through trivia, and values time spent with family and friends. Kimberly's love for the arts is evident in her passion for live music and theater. A deep connection to nature fuels her spirit.

As a self-proclaimed foodie, Kimberly delights in culinary adventures and explores the world's diverse flavors with gusto. Her insatiable curiosity about history and other cultures fuels her desire to learn continuously.

Kimberly has recently taken up writing, a testament to her pursuit of passion and a mid-life career change. She has been attending writing workshops, honing her skills, and exploring new genres. Through her words, she wants to explore and share the depths of her experiences, bringing to life the myriad interests that have shaped her remarkable journey. Join her on this literary adventure as she continues evolving and discovering beauty in life's varied tapestry.

amazon.com/author/kimberlycordova
linkedin.com/in/kimberlyburk
goodreads.com/kbcordova
facebook.com/CordovaCons

ALSO BY KIMBERLY BURK CORDOVA

LEADERSHIP SERIES

- Turning Chaos into Gold: The Alchemy of Women's Leadership
- The Emotional Intelligence Revolution (COMING SOON)

TRAVEL SERIES

- Santa Fe Uncovered: A Local's Insight into the Heart of New Mexico
- Denver Dossier: Themed Adventures for Every Traveler

EMPOWERING SMALL BUSINESSES SERIES

- Artificial Intelligence Unleashed: An Entrepreneur's Guide to Innovation
- Augmented and Virtual Reality: Unlocking Business Potential for Entrepreneurs
- Cybersecurity for Entrepreneurs: Safeguarding Your Business from Online Threats